Reader Endorsements

"Lynn Donovan's empowering message in Spiritual Enforcer is Jesus offers repentance, redemption, and restoration from unseen evil forces deliberately attacking us and our loved ones. Lynn boldly shares personal examples from her own spiritual warfare encounters to help readers understand Satan's destructive ways. Perhaps the book's very best gift is the practical advice for triumphantly tapping into the authority granted to us in Christ to combat sin, protect those we love, and replace suffering and pain with blessings. I believe this book is a must-read for every Christian desperate for victory over darkness, salvation for those we love, and a more joyful, fulfilling walk with Christ."

—**Kayla Arnesen**, *Nampa, Idaho, USA*

"This book covers a critical topic for anyone who is unequally yoked in marriage. To be effective in winning a spouse and children to Jesus, it is essential to understand spiritual warfare. In this book, Lynn takes us deep, focusing on the core issues that affect the spiritual health of a family, and bringing spiritual warfare to life with personal stories, a hope-filled approach, a splash of humor, and practical illustrations. Read, and be forever equipped!"

—**Ann Hutchison**, *Director of Spiritually Unequal Marriage, NZ*

"Thank you, Lynn, for yet another powerful book! I could not put it down! I appreciate your teachings, training, hope, love, wisdom and enthusiasm that can and will prepare a whole army of believers to pray their loved ones into the Kingdom! This book added tools to my toolbelt and I wear my new badge with wisdom, authority, and peace! This book was a great refresher as well to sharpen up some rusty tools on my belt as well."

—*Ann Marie Mora, Author, My Child Sees Monsters, Wildomar, CA, USA*

∽

"This book is exactly what I needed at the exact right time in my faith walk. So many questions I had were answered and in a way that I could comprehend. Lynn has a clear and straightforward style that is truly a gift.

I feel this book is three books in one. I went through it 3 times! The first read is a breath of air straight through to the end, the second read is to mark all the prayers and prayer prompts, the third read is to notate all of the points to use and apply to my life. I know this book will become an integral part of my faith education. I highly recommend it to anyone who is ready to have their eyes opened. No more being blinded by the enemy. No more!"

—*Karen Sadler, Clovis, CA, USA*

∽

"I couldn't stop reading this book! It is the best that Lynn Donovan has written! It's a "self-help-bible-based-do-it-yourself-demon-slaying-victory-winning book" like no other. I learned some new prayer points as well as clarification regarding strategies within my unequally yoked marriage. Everyone who reads this will want their bible, notebook and the Holy Spirit sitting next to them as they strategize with the tools you've given! Victory is ours!"

—*Barbara Twigg, Jensen Beach, FL, USA*

∽

"This book is for anyone who is seeking to truly engage the spiritual world from a Christian perspective. It goes deeper into spiritual issues than most churches would ever consider, and the education it provides is solid and simple, though challenging, and accessible to ordinary people. Lynn Donovan lays out a penetrating discussion of Christian victory and the enemy we engage with. A robust testament to all her years of study and the hard lessons she has had to live through, this book grabs the spirit world and lays out in practical details how it operates and how to effectively and powerfully interact with it. Not for the faint of heart but definitely for those searching to understand this world of two realms that we live in, this book is going to bless thousands upon thousands of readers, raising them up into mature faiths of their own."

—*Joy Heller*, *Seattle, WA, USA*

"If you were to ask me, 'Do you know that Jesus has given you authority to use His name to fight back and destroy the forces of the demonic?' I would answer, 'Yes, it's written in the Bible:'

> *Behold, I give you the authority to trample on serpents and scorpions, and over all the power of the enemy, and nothing shall by any means hurt you. Nevertheless do not rejoice in this, that the spirits are subject to you, but rather rejoice because your names are written in heaven.* —Luke 10:19–20 (NKJV)

If you were to ask me, 'Do you know what those evil forces are and how to claim victory over them in Jesus's name?'

I would have to reply, 'I am not so sure about that. I haven't been taught that in all my years of church attendance.'

In her book, *Spiritual Enforcer*, Lynn defines what those forces are that invade our lives, calling them out by name. But she doesn't leave the reader there. She takes the reader through a training program to learn what our warfare tools are and how to use them. She is equipped to do this because of her years of study and applying the Word to her and her family situations, as well as years of coaching, teaching, and praying these principles with women all of the world.

After reading *Spiritual Enforcer,* I came away ready to run the race to victory over all demonic forces. I highly recommend this book for anyone ready to dig in and learn how to walk in victory and peace."

—*Martha Bush*, *Orange, Texas, USA*

Spiritual ENFORCER

LYNN DONOVAN

THREE KEYS PUBLISHING
Books to Live By

Spiritual Enforcer
Spiritual Warfare for the Unequally Yoked
© Lynn Donovan 2024
Three Keys Publishing
6300 Puerto Drive
Rancho Murieta, CA
Threekeysministries.com

Acknowledgments

Mike Donovan, I love you. Thank you for your encouragement and support and for allowing me to share our life publicly. Your courage, self-awareness, strength, and faith inspire me every day.

Dineen Miller, your friendship and love are gifts from heaven. Thank you for your expertise and sharing your creativity with me and the world. I adore you.

Copy editor Deb Hall, thank you for making me a better author.

Thank you, Father.

"When you go out to battle against your enemies, and see horses and chariots and people more numerous than you, do not be afraid of them; for the Lord your God is with you, who brought you up from the land of Egypt (captivity).

So it shall be, when you are on the verge of battle, that the priest shall approach and speak to the people.

And he shall say to them, 'Hear, O Israel (Church): Today you are on the verge of battle with your enemies. Do not let your heart faint, do not be afraid, and do not tremble or be terrified because of them; for the Lord your God is He who goes with you, to fight for you against your enemies, to save you.'"

— Deuteronomy 20:1–4 NKJV

Ephesians 6

Take up the shield of faith, with which you can extinguish all the flmaing arrows of the evil one.

Introduction

Fight the good fight of faith, lay hold on eternal life,
to which you were also called and have confessed
the good confession in the presence of many witnesses.
—1 Timothy 6:12 (NKJV)

Welcome to the fight!

The battle for souls blazes furiously! Brothers and sisters, we are living in the end of days. And now more than any other time in modern history, we are called to such a time as this to face our enemy and fight the good fight of faith.

This book is an instructional handbook for those who are standing against evil and fighting for their mind, health, marriage, family, and the church! Within the pages are effective tactics, tools, and the truth that will empower you to battle victoriously within the spiritual realm. Your faith will be strengthened, and your power and authority in Christ will expand. You will discover that spiritual, emotional, and physical wholeness is possible for yourself and others. You will learn how to stand on the Word of God and live in a peaceful marriage as you pray for the salvation of your spouse and family. The tools contained within are mighty to the pulling down of demonic strongholds and the casting out of evil from your home.

You will develop your spiritual discernment, thereby enabling you to uncover evil plots, demonic hiding places, and ambushes that are directed toward you and your children. Great wisdom from heaven is available and will assist as you navigate the front lines. And you will walk in the triumph that was fully purchased through the atonement of Jesus, our Messiah.

I have prayed for you. I have asked our Father to bless you with divine revelation. I have petitioned heaven to help you implement a successful offensive and to set up defensive strategies with confidence and power. I've asked God to give you strength and courage as you become an "Ephesians 6 Enforcer."

And I bless you in the name of Jesus with perseverance as you lead your family and loved ones who are held captive in prisons of deception and pain. Transformative love and freedom are our destination and promised land. I have petitioned Jesus to train you and the Holy Spirit to strengthen you.

Welcome to the training ground!

Finally, my brethren, be strong in the Lord and in the power of His might. Put on the whole armor of God, that you may be able to stand against the wiles of the devil. For we do not wrestle against flesh and blood, but against principalities, against powers, against the rulers of the darkness of this age, against spiritual hosts of wickedness in the heavenly places. Therefore, take up the whole armor of God, that you may be able to withstand in the evil day, and having done all, to stand.

Stand therefore, having girded your waist with truth, having put on the breastplate of righteousness, and having shod your feet with the preparation of the gospel of peace; above all, taking the shield of faith with which you will be able to quench all the fiery darts of the wicked one. And take the helmet of salvation, and the sword of the Spirit, which is the word of God; praying always with all prayer and supplication in the Spirit, being watchful to this end with all perseverance and supplication for all the saints. —Ephesians 6:10–18 (NKJV)

Meet Lynn

Be strong and courageous.
Do not be afraid or terrified because of them,
for the Lord your God goes with you;
he will never leave you nor forsake you.
—Deuteronomy 31:6

Today, I find myself living out an unexpected mission for the kingdom of God.

Little did I realize that for most of my adult life Jesus was covertly training me to become a deliverance minister. No one is more surprised than I am. Arriving in this assignment feels accidental . . . or was it? Hmmmmm. Perhaps it was providential.

Either way, I arrived in this season of my life out of sheer necessity. You see, many years ago, I met and married my husband, Mike. When we married, I was living a prodigal life, far removed from the faith of my childhood. Three years into our marriage, that lifestyle dulled, and God called me home. Upon returning to my childhood faith, I realized in a quick minute that I was unequally yoked, and marriage was hard. Evil assaulted our relationship, home, and family, and the battles were frequent and painful.

During our first decade of marriage, I battled alone. It was only Jesus and me. I faced conflicts that left me bruised and at times spiritually bleeding. But over time, I learned to push back against the evil forces bent on destroying my marriage. The battle weaponry I gained wasn't clubs and sharp words but love, coupled with complete dependence upon

Jesus and the Word of God. As I grew up in my faith, the victories in our marriage occurred with greater frequency. Year upon year, then decade upon decade, led to the pinnacle day, our twenty-seventh wedding anniversary. On that day my husband walked into church and was baptized into the Christian faith. I've written about my marriage for nearly two decades, so as a kiss of love from the Lord, Mike confessed his belief in Jesus on our anniversary. God is so cool like that.

I'm teary eyed as I recall the faithfulness of God throughout the changing seasons of our marriage.

Today I find myself in a mature and strong faith season. Hallelujah!

Through education, experience, trial and error, and sheer revelation, I've gained a tremendous amount of spiritual warfare strategies. And because these strategies and prayers really work, I'm determined to share them with you, the unequally yoked who are walking the road a few steps behind me. The information, lessons, and battle plans drawn from my years of experience standing against the demonic are powerful and effective. The strategies I share in this book are not widely known nor discussed in wider Christian circles. However, they should be because without these concepts and instruction, God's people remain vulnerable and oppressed with some becoming prisoners of war.

The tactics are hard-fought truths. The concepts are biblical, practical, and powerful. It's good stuff!

I'm convinced that my husband's faith decision came about because I learned to battle for him and our marriage in the spiritual realm. And although my husband came to faith, we remain a good distance apart in our faith walk. After all, I've been a woman of faith for decades while my husband is merely beginning his journey. Yet today we are happily married and living the peaceful and abundant life Jesus spoke of in John 10:10. I remain committed to prayer for greater encounters between Mike and Jesus and for me too. Because it's a blast living the believer's life!

I am a pastor, teacher, speaker, author of *Winning Him Without Words, Winning Them With Prayer and Raising Godly Kids in a Spiritually Mismatched Marriage* as well as *Marching Around Jericho*, another warfare book. I've written a few other titles you can find at the end of the book. I am also a ministry leader of the SUMite Nation (spiritual-lyunequalmarriage.com), an organization of thousands who gather online to learn to fight, believe, and thrive in their unequally yoked marriages. However, the ministry work that thrills my heart over all else is healing prayer and deliverance. I was made to fight for others and for the kingdom of God.

And so are you.

So, let's determine today to step out of the enemy's grasp and enforce the will of Christ here on earth. I offer this guide as a love offering to our Father and to you, my brothers and sisters.

From the most sacred and tender part of my heart, I extend genuine encouragement from the Scriptures and real-life application of God's principles that have worked for me. I know that if you apply these tools and truths, you will also live in greater victory through Christ Jesus. I carry genuine affection for you in my heart and tremendous hope for your faith and future.

The fight is red hot. And now it's your turn to volunteer for service. The strategies, prayers, and tools defeat fear, cast out worthlessness, and shackle the voices of loathing, shame, and rejection. And the love of Christ is revealed in greater measure. Lives, relationships, and futures are restored, redeemed, and transformed.

Love is our superpower.

Our war cry is victory.

Join me. Sign up now. The battle rages, but the ending is written. Absolute triumph!

Thank you, courageous recruit. I invite you to stand alongside me for the kingdom of God. We join forces with Christ to rescue the unsaved, the broken, and the oppressed. It is my earnest prayer that the training will polish your armor and intensify your weaponry. I pray you are equipped, your authority established, and you are prepared to fight for your spouse, your marriage, and your house. I pray, in the name of Jesus, that the battle against the devil and his minions results in a resounding victory. I pray that your tremendous victory impacts a thousand generations of your family. May they prosper in the wake of your intercession. Finally, I bless you to live from the source of the peace and love, Jesus Christ, and walk in wisdom that is our birthright as children of God.

Cadet, your commissioning is at hand.

Sound the war cry!

Lynn Donovan

Ephesians 6

Take up the shield of faith, with which you can extinguish all the flmaing arrows of the evil one.

Part One
Power and Authority

For in Christ all the fullness of the Deity lives in bodily form, and in Christ you have been brought to fullness. He is the head over every power and authority. —Colossians 2:9–10

Chapter One
STAND

Put on the whole armor of God, that you may be able to stand against the wiles of the devil. —Ephesians 6:11

On most mornings I walk-n-pray with God. As I meander among the oak trees surrounding my Northern California home, I experience God in the peaceful beauty of his creation. I smile and whisper thanks when catching sight of a doe and her fawn as they forage for greenery. I'm obsessed with deer watching, which makes me happy. It's the best part of my day, loving God in tranquility.

I began my morning walks with God decades ago when I lived in Southern California. I would drive to a parking lot, not far from my house, that let out onto a country road and walk the trails among the vineyards. I remember a specific occasion several years ago when the November air was unusually warm. The morning sky reflected sapphire, calm and clear. However, I was anything but peaceful.

As I stepped onto the gravel road, turmoil rose up and confronted me again. For months now, this beast was my morning escort. Tears and fears brimmed as I struggled to keep my prayers from collapsing into panic. What I'd hoped would be my husband's short-term unemployment was stretching into six months. And his prospect of gaining full-time employment appeared remote.

I wonder, have you ever prayed panic prayers? You know, *Help me, Jesus. Help me, Jesus. Help me, Jesus.*

As I've grown up in the Lord, I've come to learn that God hears our panic prayers. However, panic prayers aren't nearly as effective as believing prayers. But after my husband's long unemployment, I found myself in a serious spiritual battle, contending for a job for him.

I find it interesting that the devil discovers where to assault the vulnerability in our minds. My vulnerability is linked to financial security. I've battled the poverty spirit for most of my life. Ugh!

On this particular day as I walked along the road and prayed for help, I looked beseechingly upward, hoping for some kind of reply. When I glanced up, I spotted something utterly peculiar in the sky. I knew immediately what I saw was of God. He was responding to my numerous petitions.

Three dots and a dash: . . . —

They were clouds. Three perfectly round clouds followed by a long, perfectly straight line. I whispered aloud, "Three dots and a dash?"

I mumbled to God. "What's this all about?"

Now, I'm not a person to read much into the clouds. Rather, I turn my heart and spirit to listen to the Lord's voice. But this time, it was so remarkable that these perfectly shaped clouds were present in an otherwise cloudless sky. I was astonished. This was unlike anything I'd ever seen.

Lord, what does this mean? I prayed.

I was perplexed looking at these perfectly shaped clouds. I was intrigued. Did you know that our Father delights in leading us as we search for understanding regarding the curious and unique (Proverbs 25:2)? And indeed, on this morning, in response to my question, I heard his prompt reply in my mind, *Look it up.*

I whipped my phone from my pocket. I couldn't type the words into the browser fast enough. Three dots and a dash: . . . —

I gasped as I stared at the screen. The top response: Morse code. Three dots and a dash translate to "V," meaning "victory"! The article

4

went on to explain that this was the exact code relayed to the battlefronts signaling the end of World War II.

The War Is Over!

Immediately I heard in my mind the song "The War Is Over," the words echoing over and over in my mind. Hallelujah! God was proving to me that victory was at hand in response to the petitions I'd been piling up before the throne of grace. My fears disappeared, and I took a stance of peace and assurance while I waited for God to move. And indeed, Mike started a new job not long after that.

My friend, it's incredibly refining, and difficult, to stand in faith when our prayers remain unanswered for months and months, let alone years and years. However, it's the positioning of our faith that ultimately leads us to victory.

Victory is obtained and enforced through our stance.

Standing in Faith

I don't know about you, but when calamity arrives, I'm compelled to "do" something. I want to jump into a plan—any plan—especially when desperate thoughts of "what if" are plaguing my mind.

How will we pay the mortgage? Wait, how will I buy groceries next week? Will this unemployment lead to bankruptcy? Will we ever get ahead?

Perhaps it's because of my personality that I initially contemplate imminent disaster.

My dear friend, let me ask you, when the "what ifs" arise in your mind, do they result in depression, immobility, or crippling fear? Well, what I've learned is that every "what if" we entertain is merely a ruse of the enemy. These thought patterns are typically a planned assault intended to derail our faith, create chaos, and turn us away from the safety of our Lord. This strategy of the devil is as old as time. It's a tiring tactic but remains effective.

However, the lifelong battle for our mind is terminated when we learn to stand.

*Therefore put on the full armor of God, so that when the day of evil comes, you may be able to stand your ground, and **after you have done everything, to stand.** —Ephesians 6:13*

Standing in the full armor of God is the most powerful position from which to fight . . . and to rest. Yes, it's possible to rest, be at peace, as we battle. Standing in faith is the position whereby we receive powerfully answered prayers, deliverance, and freedom for ourselves and our family. Also, enforcing the truths of God in the realm of the Spirit requires a stance that is immovable and defensible but also avails a viable tactical offense.

Effective warfare begins with faith, standing in faith. And our enemy, the devil, is relentless to destroy our faith and deceive us through his most successful assault: lying.

The largest part of our faith journey is unraveling lies we've believed about ourselves and God. This is the relentless battle for our mind and for truth. Learning to believe God's truth consistently protects us from deception, error, and demonic assault. This is the "stance," the spiritual position, of a kingdom enforcer!

Standing strong in the fight requires us to erect a fortified defensive posture. Developing this posture is similar to building a house. This house, our spiritual house, is established upon two grand-foundational pillars. The pillars are the sturdy structures, the *Rock* that remains immovable and trustworthy throughout the years and withstands every arrow the Enemy shoots our way.

Our foundational pillars are *intimacy* and *identity*.

Consistent and vibrant intimacy with God establishes wisdom in our choices, a strong character, and a hopeful future. Our daily interactions with Father, Son, and Holy Spirit empower us to pray with belief that moves mountains (Mark 11:23). Hearing the voice of God is a gift that's immeasurable. His words of love, wisdom, and counsel offer us every opportunity to succeed. I cannot overstate the essential need for daily time with God, listening to his voice, reading the Word, prayer, worship, and offering our willing obedience.

The blueprint for living our highest and best life is contained in the Bible. When we finally get out of our own way and truly lean into God's advice, many aspects of life become easier—simpler is perhaps a better description. A willing commitment to pursue holiness, purity, love, and God above all else are the keys to a life of fulfillment and purpose.

The second foundational pillar of our spiritual house is identity. When we identify as a child of God, we know that we know in our knower who we are in Christ. Developed identity is the core of our strong stance. Equally important is grasping the true character of the Father, Son, and Spirit. Out of our intimate knowing of God, we establish the bedrock of our great power and authority in the spiritual realm. Gaining this wisdom takes effort, and it will require challenges to poor theology as well as determined prayer seeking truth and revelation in order to unwind distortions in our faith.

Developing a strong identity requires our willing invitation, asking Jesus into our pain, seeking his healing touch of past trauma, as well as trusting him with our fears about the future. This process requires steadfast determination. Breaking agreements with lies regarding identity will require Bible study and at times the study of books written by men and women of God. This process requires tenacity and intentionality to push through the healing process. However, if you want answered prayer, miracles, power, and authority, this is required work for every kingdom enforcer. Making the effort, dedicating the time, and processing in prayer creates a house with pillars of bedrock which *stands* firm. All of hell *will not* topple your house or God's plans for your life.

Jesus said: "Therefore whoever hears these sayings of Mine, and does them, I will liken him to a wise man who built his house on the rock: and the rain descended, the floods came, and the winds blew and beat on that house; and it did not fall, for it was founded on the rock. —Matthew 7:24–25 (NKJV)

This process may feel like work, but it's also joyful and it is divine. It is healing. Intimacy is a journey overflowing with nuances of God's wonder as he reveals himself through everyday events, his goodness, and his boundless love.

Effective combat of evil begins and rests upon our intimacy with the Father, Son, and Spirit. Out of intimacy we discern God's voice in his Word, in nature, and in many other aspects of living. Thus, we grow in our understanding of the Father's character and his desires for our lives and in our understanding of humanity. We learn to align with God's principles, becoming Christlike. Time with God creates trust, which builds our confidence. Therefore, we stand in our confident positioning knowing which course of action is the best for the circumstances at hand.

For me, establishing these two faith pillars in my life was a process. I write about this journey and share the tools I gained from the "march" around my husband in my first warfare book, *Marching Around Jericho*. I detail the discovery of my true kingdom identity and of God as my good Father. I also share how my journey of faith impacted my husband's salvation. Because I've already written about intimacy and identity in my previous warfare book, I won't delve further into those details and teaching in this book.

Throughout this journey, we are building upon our strong faith and core beliefs as we continue to mature in our walk with God. The *new* tools I share with you in this book are extreme. They w*ill* defeat the demonic attacks against our homes and spouses, as well as attacks that come from multiple other sources such as witchcraft, curses, and sin.

We are building a *great* house that sits upon the Rock of Faith. Everything from this point forward—our warfare tactics, prayers, reading Scripture, and beliefs—stand upon our pillars of faith: identity and intimacy.

Compatriot, the devil's defeat is sealed! Your position is established, and the demons are quaking in fear.

Hallelujah!

Spiritual Enforcer

Ephesians 6

Take up the shield of faith, with which you can extinguish all the flaming arrows of the evil one.

Chapter Two
THE ACADEMY

As you go, proclaim this message: 'The kingdom of heaven has come near.' Heal the sick, raise the dead, cleanse those who have leprosy, drive out demons. Freely you have received; freely give.
—Matthew 10:7–8

What is spiritual warfare? It's a supernatural conflict in the unseen realm.

My friend, we are smack-dab in the middle of an epic fight. Whether or not we perceive or acknowledge this reality, every single person on this planet is embroiled in this ongoing combat of the ages. And those of us who become aware of this fact quickly realize we need to armor up and start fighting back.

For years, I lived in a Christian church community with really great people who loved Jesus. I attended Sunday services and Bible studies, but my "real life," not my Sunday morning life, rarely aligned with what was possible as described in the pages of the Bible. Instead, I felt as though I was a puppet controlled by a maniacal puppet master. Disaster, ruin, and pain were continual visitors in my home, within my marriage, and upon our finances.

For many years, I was clueless regarding the clash of powers that blazed around me and the great havoc it wreaked in nearly every area of my life. Once I finally reconciled this reality, I became desperate to learn how to deflect the wickedness directed my way and to defend myself. I also realized my spouse was unable to fulfill his role as the spiritual protector of the family, as he wasn't a believer. Therefore, this responsibility defaulted to me. I bore the lone responsibility of fighting evil for both of us *and* for our kids. In complete transparency, accepting this unfair truth was bitter and difficult. I have a strong sense of justice and fairness. I complained to God that it wasn't reasonable to expect me to do all the fighting, praying, and interceding. And it certainly wasn't fair that my husband received the benefits without any effort on his part. *Humph!*

So, yeah, I bet you know how the Lord responded to my complaints. He simply asked a question: *If you don't fight for your marriage and children, who will?* I acquiesced and somewhat coarsely accepted my commissioning into the Lord's academy of kingdom enforcers.

What began as a begrudged mission eventually became my life's passion and assignment.

And now my friend, God is asking you the same question: *Are you willing to fight for your marriage and family?*

Are you tired of losing ground and ready to be cut loose from the maniacal puppet master? Think about it. You are already in the war. Would you like to take back your life, thoughts, and future? How about your church, city, even your nation, for God's purposes and glory?

Somewhere deep inside, listen as your soul whispers yes.

Congratulations! Today, you are accepted into Yeshua's Academy of Elite Demon Assassins. Cool title, don't you think?

My friend, it's a heavy journey, but every sacrifice of your personal time, along with the hours of prayers and petitions, will result in miracles of healing, manifestations of deliverance, and a life of freedom from fear and condemnation.

You get Jesus!

How do I know? This is what happened to me.

The first part of our journey is already written. We know we are participants in an epic battle for our earthly lives as well as for eternities of souls. We know victory is certain as we will discover that the atonement provided every tool needed for enforcement and successful living. This next part of our journey is destined to be different from what we have lived until now. We will learn real enforcement of God's law and live in the abundance of his grace and goodness.

As disciples, Jesus has issued our mandate. Love God. Love People. And from this place we are commissioned to share the good news, heal the sick, cleanse the lepers, cast out demons, and raise the dead. He's not joking around. This is a real mandate, and I am expectant that we will behold the fulfillment of this mandate and make it commonplace in our daily lives.

Recruit, let's learn how we become members of this elite team.

An Ordinary Believer

Heal the sick, cleanse the lepers, raise the dead, cast out demons. Freely you have received, freely give. —Matthew 10:8

I used to think this passage in the book of Matthew only applied to "Super Christians." You know, those articulate and captivating preachers and teachers who stand on a stage before thousands. After all, it was obvious to me that Super Christians are the right kind of people God would use to bring someone back from the dead?

Well, I'm not a Super Christian. I am not like preachers who are comfortable in the pulpit or on television and social media. I'm just ordinary. I'm a regular, everyday believer who struggles to figure out what to cook for dinner. I have beds to make and toilets to clean. Yep, that's me.

Yet can you believe it? Jesus teaches this passage as though it's available to everyday, ordinary toilet cleaners just like me . . . and you.

A Regular Toilet Cleaner

A few months ago, I attended a local gathering of ladies from around my neighborhood. We regularly meet for lunch and to enjoy a speaker or entertainment. It's an opportunity to build friendships with women who live nearby.

Well, on this specific morning, before I'd showered and dressed for the event, I sat with my coffee, my Bible, and the Lord during my morning prayer time. While I was spending time with God, a thought dropped into my head that someone might faint and fall flat out on the floor. And if that were to happen, I should place my hand on her head and say, "You shall live and not die."

Weird!

I didn't think much about that random thought at the time, and it quickly faded from my conscious.

However, a few hours later, while seated at a table waiting for the festivities to begin, an older woman who was walking across the room did indeed pass out. She fell flat out on the floor. A small chaos erupted as people jumped to their feet to watch and help. Someone called emergency services, and people began to circle around her motionless body.

Instantly, I knew exactly what was going on. God loved this woman, and premature death is never his idea. It wasn't a mere coincidence the Holy Spirit had dropped that thought into my brain earlier in the morning. So, I stood up and walked over to where she was on the floor. Others were holding her hands, and someone was on the phone with the dispatcher. I leaned over and observed that the woman's eyes were completely rolled up into her head. I perceived she wasn't breathing. It didn't look good.

Lord, Jesus, could this really be happening?

I gently placed my hand on the top of her head and spoke aloud but not loudly, "You shall live and not die." I stood. I waited, prayed in tongues under my breath a moment, but no response. I bent down again with my hand on her head. This time I spoke with more force and volume, "You shall live and not die!"

Immediately, the woman's pupils rolled down and back into place. She regained consciousness instantly.

I smiled and said in a joyful voice to those around us, "There she is." I knew she was going to be okay. I stood up and returned to my seat, praying quietly, "Thank you, Jesus. Thank you, Jesus. Praise you, Jesus. I love you, Jesus." Upon returning to my table, I told the woman seated next to me that God told me this exact incident would happen and that God provided specific details and instructions for me. And that the woman was going to be okay.

She stared at me intently and said, "You just gave me chill bumps. You really knew that?"

"Yes, God told me, and he told me what to do."

The EMTs arrived, and they whisked the somewhat shaken but fully conscious woman off to the hospital.

Just an Ordinary Day

Did I really participate in something so uncanny and miraculous?

Yep, this is just an ordinary day in the life of a believer who has determined to partner with the Holy Spirit. There were about 150 guests in that room that morning, and it's likely that not one of them knew that God saved that woman's life. But I know. And all those watching from the unseen realm, they also know.

When I recall this event and the great love God has for people, I'm undone. I was privileged to be the hands and feet of Jesus to accomplish his good works on earth. Hallelujah!

Cadet, this is an example of an ordinary believer, living the extraordinary Christian life. Our broken, hurting, and ill-stricken world needs us. Our families need us. Jesus is pleading with his church to step up and use his power and authority to love people and change outcomes.

The Academy Is Open

The Bible likens spiritual warfare to a military construct. Instead of military battles, let's take a more modern approach. Let's consider engagements with evil from an enforcement perspective. We will train in kingdom enforcement as a new academy recruit.

Similar to a police academy, as a cadet in training, we will apply ourselves to study and knowledge. Eventually we will practice our skills and finally graduate. We become badged officers. From there we step into areas of interest and giftedness, eventually specializing in such areas as tactics, demon assassins, undercover rescue agents, SWAT team intercessors, and more. As we work our way through the training, our aptitude and gifting will lead us into areas of unique ability and confidence.

Pray this aloud today and write the date next to this prayer in the margin. This is your commitment and launch. Your words are honored by all of heaven.

Father, in the name of Jesus, today I dedicate myself to serving your kingdom wholeheartedly with all of my mind, soul, and strength. I am determined to walk in the authority of Christ and in the power of the Holy Spirit. I am determined to bring your kingdom to earth as it is in heaven by sharing the good news of your life and ministry. I will also share your love, healing, and truth. You can count on me to be a person who releases life. Begin to move quickly in my life, establish me as a strong house, built upon Jesus, the Rock. Thank you, Jesus, for choosing me to reveal your love to a lost and broken world.

In the mighty name of Jesus. Amen.

Ephesians 6

Take up the shield of faith, with which you can extinguish all the flaming arrows of the evil one.

Chapter Three
AUTHORITY IN CHRIST

Then the seventy returned with joy, saying, "Lord, even the demons are subject to us in Your name." And He said to them, "I saw Satan fall like lightning from heaven. Behold, I give you the authority *to trample on serpents and scorpions, and* over all the power of the enemy, *and nothing shall by any means hurt you. Nevertheless do not rejoice in this, that the spirits are subject to you, but rather rejoice because your names are written in heaven."* —Luke 10:17–20 (NKJV, emphasis mine)

Enlistment

I perceived eyes opposing me. Aghast, I stared back.

My mind swirled as Mike and I continued to argue back and forth across his home-office desk. Our words were gaining in volume and frustration. As we argued, I stared at the malevolent eyes looking at me from behind my husband's eyes. I observed these glinting eyes were enjoying our escalating anger and contentious words. I quickly reconciled this was a dark and cunning presence. It was mocking me. It mocked both of us. As I watched, I realized I wasn't quarreling with my husband. This was something else.

Now, I know the Bible teaches that we don't fight against flesh and blood but against principalities, powers, and rulers. We know this to be true because accounts of demonic deliverances exist throughout the Gospels. One third of Jesus's ministry was freeing people from demons.

However, it's an altogether different story when you know the demon is in your house and arguing with you through your husband. Sheesh! This encounter brought into sharp focus my need to understand my spiritual authority, of which I knew little at the time. Watching this evil creature laugh at us, I realized I didn't know how to stop it from creating havoc in my home. And the reality struck me that it was time to face my own demons, such as fear, anger, and disappointment. It was up to me to gain my freedom and grow in my authority in Christ; then I could effectively fight for my husband.

This pivotal experience launched me into study, practice, and growing my authority in Christ.

Authority in Christ

Then Jesus came to them and said, "All authority in heaven and on earth has been given to me. —Matthew 28:18

The best way to comprehend our authority over the demonic realm is to understand the authority of Jesus. Take a look at Matthew 28:18. Our Father in heaven bestowed all authority to Jesus. All really means *all*. Now read Luke 10:17–20. Jesus passes his dominion, all authority, to his disciples, including his modern-day disciples. That's us!

What is this authority? In Matthew 28:18, when translated from the Greek, the word *authority* is "exousia." This definition is used in terms of a moral influence, dominion, or jurisdiction over a realm, right, privilege, or ability.

So how do we gain our authority in Christ? Let's think of it in this context. Consider my next-door neighbor, Dan. He's a regular sort of guy. He likes golfing and working in his yard. He attends church and spends time with family and friends on the weekend. He is a good neighbor, a good citizen. He's an ordinary man, who lives in the neighborhood.

However, on Monday morning, Dan opens his closet and takes out his law enforcement uniform. He carefully dresses to code, dons his bullet proof vest (protection), baton and gun (show of force), and radio (communication, prayer). Next, he does something extraordinary. He affixes his badge to his chest. From this moment forward, he now carries the full enforcement authority of the principal government (kingdom) as he polices his territory (his jurisdiction).

Our authority in Christ is like putting on a badge. We step into the ultimate authority with a badge on our chest that demons, angels, and the entire spiritual realm respects. The problem is that half the time, Christians don't realize they are wearing this powerful badge. They don't understand the implications, good and bad, or the absolute authority of the power of the possessor. They are unaware of the spiritual and physical jurisdictions that belong to them that must be defended. And most regrettably, they are oblivious to everything that is available to them as Christ's enforcers in the unseen realm.

Our first and primary required training as a cadet is apprehending our badge, our authority in Christ. Next, we step into the reality that our success in the spirit realm is firmly established. Christ's atonement provides everything we need for an offensive and defensive stand. We literally, and I mean *literally*, are empowered to move a mountain. It is absolutely possible to defeat every foe and live an abundant life.

So, if this is true, why are many believers lacking in authority?

The simple answer: our faith must mature. This is why the apostle Paul urges believers to grow up.

Brothers and sisters, I could not address you as people who live by the Spirit but as people who are still worldly—mere infants in Christ. I gave you milk, not solid food, for you were not yet ready for it. Indeed, you are still not ready. You are still worldly. *For since there is jealousy and quarreling among you, are you not worldly? Are you not acting like mere humans? —1 Corinthians 3:1–3 (emphasis mine)*

When I teach on the topic of our authority in Christ, the audience always raises the question, How do I gain greater authority in Christ? This isn't the right question. We already possess all authority in Christ. So, the correct questions are the following:

- In what areas in my life am I lacking spiritual maturity or lacking faith, or belief?
- What lies am I believing about myself or about God? What do I fear?
- What are the open doors that allow demonic access into my house (both my spiritual house and my physical house)?

Belief = Faith

Maturation of our faith opens greater realms of spiritual authority. I want you to comprehend this next statement, as it is foundational to successful warfare. *What we truly believe is what will manifest.* Good and bad. Belief is faith. Jesus confirms this: "Therefore I tell you, whatever you ask for in prayer, *believe* that you have received it, and it will be yours" (Mark 11:24, emphasis mine).

Every word in the Bible is absolutely true. It is the very voice of God, and within it holds the truths written for us that we may live a powerful life. So here is the most powerful tool to carry with you always as an enforcer:

Know the Word of God and believe it.

Period. The end.

Obviously, I know. However, I cannot overemphasize the power of belief. Take time, search it out for yourself, and become fully convinced the Bible is the inerrant Word of God. It is the blueprint for wholehearted living. When we pray out of the desires of God's heart, nothing is impossible or out of reach.

And hear me now, this is not a name-it-and-claim-it gospel. I don't believe in that. What I'm sharing is straight from the Word of God, the voice of Jesus. I have actually lived this out in my life. *The key to authority is aligning your life to God's voice and his heart.*

Now faith is confidence in what we hope for and assurance about what we do not see. This is what the ancients were commended for. —Hebrews 11:1–2

Attaining greater authority in Christ begins with belief. It's our confident expectation that when we pray, speaking to a mountain that must move, we are convinced God hears and he will respond. Our confidence is derived from our ongoing and intimate relationship with him. We pray from the familiarity of knowing God's heart and his Word. Therefore, when we pray in accordance with his will and purposes, he is exceedingly anxious to respond to prayers birthed from a mature and surrendered heart. God is aware that mature believers are trustworthy and are rarely careless with his power and authority.

Add to belief a life of quick obedience, finally choosing faith over fear and doubt. This is the process of transforming the mind mentioned in Romans.

Do not conform to the pattern of this world, but be transformed by the renewing of your mind. *Then you will be able to test and approve what God's will is—his good, pleasing and perfect will. —Romans 12:2 (emphasis mine)*

Changing My Mind

Mike was unemployed, and again we faced another unexpected financial crisis. The enemy always aims at our vulnerability. Ugh! Ask yourself, Where are the areas in my life that are consistently or frequently under strain, attack, or defeat? This is a great place to search for lies, open doors, and places where the devil may have inroads into your beliefs.

Following an initial job interview, Mike was a promising candidate. He was merely waiting for an offer of employment to arrive. However, the offer didn't arrive. And didn't arrive. Still didn't arrive. And what should have taken two weeks stretched on into the summer. Without an offer in hand, new applications were completed. Interviews came and went until finally all opportunities dried up and months of unemployment appeared inevitable. We needed a miracle. We were facing the reality of losing our brand-new home of three months.

During this summer, every morning as I awoke and conscious thought returned, the cold hand of dread gripped my mind. Thoughts of ruin clouded my brain, and fear sat like a rock in the pit of my stomach. I would rise and struggle to push back the fear through sheer force of my will. Gathering my coffee and Bible, I headed to the backyard patio to pray. I prayed through Mark 11 nearly every day, reasserting my firm belief and speaking into the spiritual realm, commanding the mountain of unemployment to be removed and cast into the sea.

> *When evening came, Jesus and his disciples went out of the city.*
>
> *In the morning, as they went along, they saw the fig tree withered from the roots. Peter remembered and said to Jesus, "Rabbi, look! The fig tree you cursed has withered!"*
>
> *"Have faith in God," Jesus answered. "Truly I tell you, if anyone says to this mountain, 'Go, throw yourself into the sea,' and does not doubt in their heart but believes that what they say will happen, it will be done for them. Therefore I tell you, whatever you ask for in prayer, believe that you have received it, and it will be yours. —Mark 11:19–24*

In this passage Jesus is revealing the key to our authority. First, have faith in God. This means believe God is good and has good for you. Believe he is all-powerful and available to help you in every circumstance. Believe he is a loving Father and desires a good life and good things for you. Simply believe in the God of the Bible.

Second, we are instructed to speak to our mountain. As sons and daughters of God, our words carry great power. And that is what I was doing each morning that summer. The Bible is filled with passages that affirm the power of our faith, our belief, and our spoken words.

> *The tongue has the power of life and death. —Proverbs 18:21*

> *For by your words you will be acquitted, and by your words you will be condemned. —Matthew 12:37*

Spiritual Enforcer

Do not let any unwholesome talk come out of your mouths, but only what is helpful for building others up according to their needs, that it may benefit those who listen. —Ephesians 4:29

Whoever would love life and see good days must keep their tongue from evil and their lips from deceitful speech. —1 Peter 3:10

We assert our voice and command loudly with gusto: "Mountain, be removed! Be cast into the sea. In Jesus's name." Remember, all of our authority is in and through Christ. And Jesus instructs us to ask in his name.

And I will do whatever you ask in my name, so that the Father may be glorified in the Son. You may ask me for anything in my name, and I will do it. —John 14:13-14

Then believe, or as Jesus said, "Do not doubt in your heart."

This sounds simple, but here is where the real fight ensues. We must face down the distortions and lies and our own unbelief. We must stare fear in the face and demand that it leaves.

There were a number of mornings I would sit on the patio with my Bible and simply state, out loud, over and over again, "I will not partner with fear. I will not partner with doubt." I would continue to command this mountain of unemployment to move. I would command fear and unbelief to leave. Then I would remind the Father that his Word says . . . (I would quote the passage back to him as well as his promises to me.) It's likely that he didn't need reminding and this prayer was mainly for my benefit.

On these warm summer mornings, as I faithfully prayed, our unemployment situation appeared bleak from my earthly view. All prospects, every possible opportunity had been absolutely exhausted. Financial disaster was imminent, but I refused to relent and believe what looked apparent.

One night, I was praying aloud into the darkened bedroom where I lay in bed, unable to sleep. I said, "Lord, we really need you. We need your help as everything is on the line. I'm tired of fighting the fear."

It was 11:30 p.m. and at that moment, God showed up.

Say what???

He asked me a question. *Lynn, what do you need?*

Oh, for goodness' sake. Didn't God know what I needed? After all, I'd been bombarding the heavens with my prayers for help for months. I was puzzled and somewhat bewildered. But I responded quietly with love in my words and stated the obvious: "Lord, Mike needs a job."

There was a pause. I waited and listened in my mind. Then, with a kind yet firm voice God asked another question: *Lynn, what do you really need?* I was confused. Wait, what was the Lord trying to reveal? I thought it was obvious what I needed. Then a thought came to my mind.

I replied, "What we really need is for our mortgage to be paid off."

That's right, Father replied.

Wow! Not once had I considered that my fears and insecurity were tied directly to the mortgage. I always thought it was unemployment. God is such a good dad. Patient and kind, revealing the true problem.

Then Father said, *Now you are getting it. Lynn, you aren't praying big enough.*

Gulp.

"I'm not?" I stumbled about in my words, a bit dumbfounded.

Our problem wasn't the lack of a job; it was the debt that was my oppressor. And this was the real mountain that had to move. I sprang out of bed and began wandering around the house as I was engaging in this stunning conversation with God. Mike asked me, "What are you doing?" I'm never up past ten.

"God is speaking to me and it's wonderful." Mike flashed that familiar half smile toward me when I tell him God is talking. He returned to his television show.

I wandered back to the bedroom as the Lord asked another question. Incidentally, when God asks questions, these are lightning moments in our lives. His questions will tweak our understanding and draw us further into truth. Questions from our Lord open us up to life-changing revelation that imparts his goodness.

So, Lynn, when I give Mike a job, and I pay off your mortgage, what are you going to do with all that money?

Immediately, from the depths of my soul, these words sprang forth: "I'm going to build an orphanage or help rescue sex-trafficked women and children."

Now you are getting it, Lynn. You are aligning with my kingdom purposes. I was overwhelmed with his joy and love and couldn't sleep for hours as I revisited the truth and love God imparted. That night I became empowered to pray for big things. And not only that, to believe for them.

The lessons in this season were many. But the most important thing I learned was God was reliable and trustworthy; he has my best interests at heart and responds to my prayers. Wow!

Finally, the last scripture in this passage of Mark 11 is interesting. It includes forgiveness. Forgiveness is a gift of freedom. When we forgive someone, ourselves, and/or God, we are released from an evil tie that binds us. It is wisdom to make an inquiry of the Lord to search out any unforgiveness in our heart and mind. This is mature faith.

Therefore I tell you, whatever you ask for in prayer, believe that you have received it, and it will be yours. And when you stand praying, if you hold anything against anyone, forgive them, so that your Father in heaven may forgive you your sins. —Mark 11:24–25

Faithfulness

Several more weeks passed as I continued to pray GIANT prayers, speaking and believing, "I will not partner with fear. I will not partner with doubt. I cast this mortgage into the sea. In Jesus's name."

On a Thursday afternoon, as I was packing my bag and preparing to leave for a speaking engagement, God responded to my faith.

I was scheduled to speak at a women's retreat where I planned to teach the lessons I'd gained from Mark 11. And wouldn't you know it, with perfect timing, an employment offer arrived in Mike's email just as I zipped up my travel bag. As it turns out, this would become the best job of Mike's career! And it came about as a result of the very first application he'd submitted nearly three months earlier.

Say what!!!

Right on time. As I was leaving to teach at a women's conference about moving a mountain, our unemployment mountain moved. Hallelujah! This was a powerful maturing process for my faith. And it was one of the best teachings I've offered an audience.

Our authority in Christ increases as our faith matures. Powerful authority is unwavering belief in the Word of God, commanding with our voice our faith actions and intentions, coupled with a steady conviction that will not partner with fear and unbelief.

I'll bet you know what mountain I am believing for today. I hope by the end of this book I will show you a photo of our Deed of Reconveyance reflecting that our home mortgage is paid in full. I'm praying and believing. In Jesus's name.

This is our sturdy faith stance; it is a positioning in the spiritual realm. We know who we are. We know whose we are. So, when a situation presents itself, we are equipped with love, compassion, and knowledge of God and his desired outcomes. Therefore, we are confident when we pray, knowing we will ask for the right thing in the moment. And finally, we act upon our faith with assurance, knowing heaven backs our intentions and words.

Let's go back to the office where Mike and I were arguing back and forth over the desk. I looked at this thing that was mocking me from behind Mike's eyes. In a simple, firm voice, I spoke, "I take authority over this fighting and command it to stop. In Jesus's name."

Mike looked at me, and we fell silent. I think he was shocked. I certainly was shocked. But I'll tell you what, the quarreling stopped. I turned and left his office. Peace followed.

Pray and Believe

Cadet, if this is the truth of the Bible, then the obvious question arises: Why isn't every prayer answered? There are a number of issues that play a role in answered prayer:

- Selfish or poor motives
- Timing
- Controlling prayers (especially control over another person's free will)
- Asking for the wrong thing
- Demonic blocks
- Unbelief
- Did I say *timing*?

God is coordinating an entire universe and overseeing billions of lives on planet Earth. Sometimes God answers immediately. He loves to encourage his kids through answered prayer. Then there are replies to prayer that require us to tarry, travail, and persist in belief. And finally, sometimes God responds to our prayer immediately but the answer/gift/provision/opportunity is stolen away or delayed by evil spirits or evil people. An example of demonic interference with an answer to prayer is found in the book of Daniel, chapter 10. Read it when you have time.

My friend, while we are in waiting for answered prayer, it's our standing in faith training that makes a difference. We stand in truth and wait with confident expectation. Quote the verse below to the Lord when you are praying in the waiting. It's a powerful reminder.

This is the confidence *we have in approaching God: that if we ask anything according to his will, he hears us. And if we know that he hears us—whatever we ask—we know that we have what we asked of him. —1 John 5:14–15 (emphasis mine)*

In the morning, Lord, you hear my voice; in the morning I lay my requests before you and wait expectantly. *—Psalm 5:3 (emphasis mine)*

Now faith is confidence *in what we* hope *for and assurance about what we do not see. —Hebrews 11:1 (emphasis mine)*

This is the power of belief!

Activate Belief

Here are several transformative scriptures to pray and believe God is moving to fulfill. Pray them aloud, and write the date next to each in the margin. Write a specific prayer request on the lines below that you are believing God for fulfillment. Pray them back to God often, in faith.

They replied, "Believe in the Lord Jesus, and you will be saved—you and your household." —Acts 16:31

Now faith is confidence in what we hope for and assurance about what we do not see. —Hebrew 11:1

For God has not given us a spirit of fear, but of power and of love and of a sound mind. —2 Timothy 1:7 NKJV

For the unbelieving husband has been sanctified through his wife, and the unbelieving wife has been sanctified through her believing husband. Otherwise your children would be unclean, but as it is, they are holy. —1 Corinthians 7:14

"I will give you the keys of the kingdom of heaven; whatever you bind on earth will be bound in heaven, and whatever you loose on earth will be loosed in heaven." —Matthew 16:19

"A new command I give you: Love one another. As I have loved you, so you must love one another. By this everyone will know that you are my disciples, if you love one another." —John 13:34–35

—Psalm 91

—Psalm 23

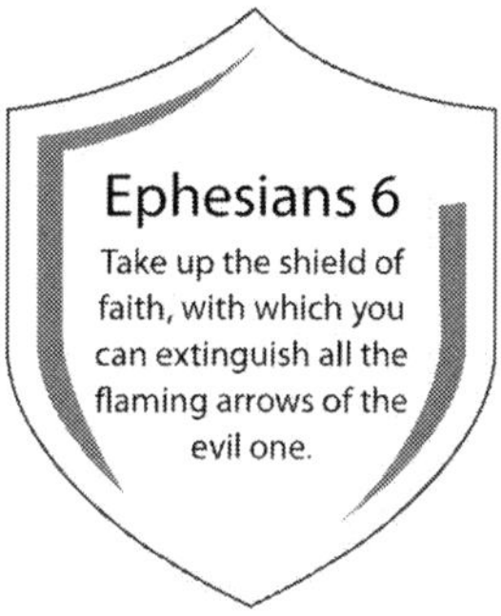

_____

_____

_____

_____

_____

_____

Ephesians 6

Take up the shield of
faith, with which you
can extinguish all the
flaming arrows of the
evil one.

Chapter Four

AUTHORITY IN THE HOUSE

Then Jesus came to them and said, "All authority in heaven and on earth has been given to me." —Matthew 28:18

C adet, are you eager to polish your badge and wear it boldly? Visualize yourself wearing a gleaming badge affixed to your chest. And believe the angelic realm is beside you to authenticate and uphold your prayers of authority through Jesus.

Now let's train to exercise our authority in our house.

Satanic agents covet our home territory as their highest prize. With this in mind, our primary mission is the daily defense against interlopers who intend to harm, afflict, kill, and destroy our physical body and our soul. The soul realm encompasses our mind, intellect, will, choices, and emotions. The next prize that evil scopes for destruction is our physical home where we live with our family. How do these marauders find a way inside in the first place? Lies.

It's important to ask yourself, *What lies am I believing about myself or God?*

Of course, this question ultimately points back to our beliefs regarding identity. I'm convinced that our entire faith journey is the process of unwinding lies as well as maturing in our identity in Christ and finally discovering the depths of God's love and his purposes on the earth.

Conflicts with evil are inevitable. I'll dare say they are necessary. Without pushback against our ideologies, beliefs, and theology, we will not mature. It's when we are in the midst of fire we learn to pray powerfully, without ceasing. When under pressure, our faith is refined; thereby we ascertain God is reliably faithful and all things are possible with Christ.

When facing financial disaster, it took all the determination I possessed to reject the devil's lies about God. You know those little thoughts of doubt that spring up to impart fear and leave us hopeless, such as *God only helps others and doesn't help me; God isn't listening to me; God doesn't answer my prayers; God loves others, but he doesn't love me; God always disappoints me.*

My friend, when these thoughts present themselves, I promise they are coming directly from a lying demon. They are a direct attack on the truth about our Father's character and about who we are as his children. This lying spirit operates subtly, convincing us these are our thoughts. The key to conquering our wandering mind is consistent practice, learning to recognize the deceptions early on, then to refuse to agree. Immediately take these thoughts captive to Christ. Remember, I would rebut the lies by speaking aloud, *I refuse to partner with doubt. I refuse to partner with fear.*

Future enforcer, as defenders of freedom there are moments when we will feel fear. Doubts will arise, creating confusion that leads to second-guessing our decisions. The devil attempts to trap us in negative thought patterns, birthing fear and unbelief. But here is the solution to fortifying your house: what you choose to do with your thoughts and feelings of fear will determine if they retain space in your house, your mind, and your life.

It's true that we will *feel* fear. However, it's in the moment, often a split second, that we will make a fundamental choice. Either we choose to believe the voice of fear and then align with it—thereby empowering the fear into reality—or we choose to partner with the truth.

Choose rightly. Partner with faith over fear, God's truth over deception.

Take errant thoughts captive by refusing to participate. Refuse to partner in the deceptions of evil. Speak out loud, "I REFUSE!" And then pick up your enforcer's weapon, the Word. Blast that demon smack in the face with it. Tell evil, "I believe in the Lord Jesus Christ. You can't have me, my thoughts, my home, or my family. You can't have my marriage, my faith, or anything that is under my love, stewardship, or jurisdiction. In the mighty name of Jesus, amen!"

For God has not given us a spirit of fear, but of power and of love and of a sound mind. —2 Timothy 1:7 NKJV

This is one of my favorite verses to defeat and destroy the enemy who is attacking. I like to use my weapon and take a demon's head off. I speak to the evil something like this:

Devil, I will not bow to fear or doubt. You know why, devil, because my Father did NOT give me a spirit of fear. Oh no, no, no, devil, he did not. You know what God gave me? He gave me a spirit of power. And I use that power right now to defeat you. I bind you right now by the Word of God in Matthew 16:19. I command you to stand down and get out of my house right now. You cannot speak to me. You cannot speak to my husband or my children. We will not come under your authority. I live under the authority of Jesus, to whom every knee bows. That means you, devil.

Devil, do you know what else God gave me? A spirit of love. I choose love. I choose love when it's easy. I choose love when it's hard. You don't even know what to do with love, devil. I am loved by God. I am loved by my family, and I love my God, myself, and my family. You cannot come against my love and that of my Father in heaven. My love defeats you right now!

And guess what, devil, my God gave me a sound mind. So, this confusion is banished from my house. You get out. I walk in steady truth, and I am assured that my decisions are sound, and my life is on course. I will

*not partner with your confusion or lies. In the powerful name of my Lord
Jesus Christ, amen!*
  Take that, devil!

I recognize this process isn't always easy. Many of us are riddled with fears and doubts that are rooted in our past experiences. The devil throws every flaming arrow at us that he can conjure up, especially when we are young, innocent, and unprotected, with the intention that some pain and fear will stick. He is well aware that unhealed pain is a potential opening for oppression.

Maturing faith is the process of facing your trauma and working through any unforgiveness. It's divorcing yourself from habitual sin. It's also a lifestyle of forgiveness and a pursuit to honor God. We often need help along the way. Most of us will need inner healing and deliverance. Others must find a way to forgive the unforgivable. But Jesus is kind and absolutely capable when taking us through healing and restoration.

I bear witness that in hundreds of healing prayer sessions I've conducted with believers, Jesus can heal a lifetime of disappointment. He restores broken hearts, restores purity, and releases people from crippling fear and unbelief. He heals our trauma and our soul. He heals our body and then blesses us in his love. He is kind and gentle, desiring our healing. He will kindly remove our hurts and fears.

Take the time to work through your healing. Get help. Get prayer support. Also, live in a community with spirit-filled believers who surround you with hope. And always be a student of the kingdom. If you need help with your healing journey, find out more about my prayer ministry in Appendix A.

Maturing as a child of God is a truly wondrous and awe-inspiring journey, yet there are also challenges. I'll promise you this: living wholeheartedly through Christ, THIS is the Father's endgame for our human experience. It is Christ's great reward to know we live the abundant life for which he paid the highest price.

When you are restored and standing in your wholeness, wearing your badge, knowing the Father is for you and Jesus is with you and the Holy Spirit abides within, the devils who are looking for victims become the tortured and afraid. When you hit your prayer closet, they are scrambling, hiding, and looking for an exit clause.

There is a photo circling around Christian social media depicting a praying mama holding a shield over her child who sits calmly on the ground. Flaming arrows are raining down aimed specifically at destroying her toddler. But the innocent little boy is completely protected and at peace because his mama prays.

I smile whenever the photo pops up in my feed.

This is a picture of the spiritual realm. Our faith protects our family. Our faith is the protection over our marriage. Our prayers are the spiritual protection over our homes.

Cadet, the Lord knew there would be unequally yoked marriages. These marital unions have been around since before Jesus walked the earth. It doesn't matter how you arrived in your marriage; the Lord desires to bless your marriage and family. He's more concerned about what you are doing today instead of a decision you made when you were younger.

> *For the unbelieving husband is sanctified by the wife, and the unbelieving wife is sanctified by the husband; otherwise your children would be unclean, but now they are holy. —1 Corinthians 7:14 NKJV*

This verse offers the truth about God's opinion and his will toward those of us in mismatched marriages. As the believing spouse, we sanctify and make holy all who live under our shield of faith. This is our protection over our home and family. This is our hope.

We do our part: grow up, pray, protect, BELIEVE. Then we watch the miracles happen. Wait, we are invited to participate with Jesus to make the miracles happen.

What a God! What a faith! What a life!

Ephesians 6

Take up the shield of
faith, with which you
can extinguish all the
flaming arrows of the
evil one.

Chapter Five
ENFORCEMENT POWER

*I have given you authority to trample on snakes and scorpions
and to overcome all the power of the enemy; nothing will harm
you. —Luke 10:19*

Cadet to Enforcement Officer

Enforcer, we have discovered our badge of authority in Jesus Christ. We have also learned how to protect and fortify our body, mind, family, and house. However, evil attacks are certain to occur, and we should expect pushback.

Today, let's discover the power we carry in Christ. Take another look at Officer Dan. In general, when Dan patrols his jurisdiction, his badge is well respected. If he detects a willful lawbreaker, he speaks to that behavior with a command to cease and desist. Most transgressors are quick to comply and discontinue their unlawful conduct. The community understands strong repercussions exist for those who breach the laws of the land. However, there are a number of evil marauders, thieves, murderers who are hell-bent on destroying life and peace and stealing anything they can get their hands on. They search for openings to steal what isn't theirs. They deceive to gain access to areas that belong to others. Through cunning, they intentionally break boundaries, irrespective of the law and enforcement patrols.

When Officer Dan discovers one of these thieves in action and the offender refuses his verbal commands to stand down, he draws his weapon. Dan is well aware that enforcement must be accompanied with a show of force. Dan's enforcement weapon is an obvious threat of injury or death. The lawbreakers know they are facing danger. They know the officer won't hesitate to use his weapon; thus, they immediately comply with the officer's command to desist.

However, on occasion an arrogant or calculating criminal will challenge Officer Dan. But Dan is authorized to discharge his firearm to serve and protect. Enforcement of societal law is upheld and obeyed because Officer Dan is empowered to use his weapon.

Cadet, there must exist a strong show of force for effective protection.

This is the power behind the badge.

This analogy applies to the spiritual realm. As believers, our courageous willingness to exercise our power to enforce our authority is highly respected in the unseen realm. Christ's authority is our badge, and the Holy Spirit and angelic forces are the power, or the enforcer's gun, that backs our authority.

Evil spirits are relentless in their activity to breach our protective boundaries. They search for legal loopholes as well as illegal means to enter our personal house, our body, and our soul in an attempt to destroy and kill us through sickness and disease, both mental and physical. Tirelessly they toil with brutal intent to violate our physical dwelling where we live with our family. They use our unsaved spouse and others, who are influenced by their voices of lies, to create confusion, pain, and destruction.

However, in Christ we are more than conquerors. He has empowered us to fight for ourselves and others. Jesus models this concept throughout the Gospels. His deliverance ministry was a demonstration of power and authority over evil. He exerted power to cast out the Gadarene demoniac, save the boy who was plagued by seizures, and raise a young girl from the dead. It's the same for us. When we partner with the Holy Spirit, we exercise our heavenly nature through our prayers, words of command, and faith to bind, kick out, and destroy demonic activity. We exert our power and authority in Christ into our reality through our identity, our faith, and our voice.

So, what does this look like? Glad you asked.

Several years ago, I was plagued by joint pain in my hands. My fingers were swollen and sore. My fingers crackled often because of worsening stiffness. It was impossible for me to tuck my thumbs in and touch the palms of my hands. I was annoyed.

It was the onset of arthritis. As a young woman I watched my grandmother's hands gnarl and knot from the inflammation and pain that attacked her. It's a generational disease in my family.

When the doctor confirmed my suspicions and told me medicine wouldn't reverse the curse, I got mad! Not at the doctor.

I was mad at the devil. I decided there was *no way* I would accept this diagnosis or the disease in my body. So I began to pray. I knew that restrictive diseases like arthritis are often spiritually linked to unforgiveness, resentment, and bitterness. I prayed and asked the Lord if there was anyone I hadn't forgiven. I mentally went through any and all names of people I might need to forgive. I confessed and renounced any and all resentment and any lingering bitterness. I did this all again even though I'd prayed through these issues in previous years. But I wanted to be certain that the demonic realm didn't have a legal right to afflict me.

Then I prayed and used my authority to command arthritis, along with any evil spirit behind it, to *get out*! And get out now. In Jesus's name. I remember for several weeks I would consistently pray and command all resentment, bitterness, unforgiveness out. I commanded all pain and inflammation to get out immediately. I commanded out anything and everything that came to mind. In Jesus's name.

I blessed my hands with healing and wholeness. I blessed them to be pain free and to move easily. I blessed them with divine health and the love of Jesus. I blessed them to be hands that bring God's goodness to people. I bless them today to type freely as I work on this book. In Jesus's name.

And you know what? Within a few weeks my hands were pain free. I no longer have cracking knuckles, and both thumbs easily touch the palms of my hands.

I am healed in Jesus's name. Hallelujah. Thank you, Jesus!

Let's take a look at another example where Jesus confronts a territorial spirit:

> Then he got into the boat and his disciples followed him. Suddenly a furious storm came up on the lake, so that the waves swept over the boat. But Jesus was sleeping. The disciples went and woke him, saying, "Lord, save us! We're going to drown!"
>
> He replied, "You of little faith, why are you so afraid?" Then he got up and rebuked the winds and the waves, and it was completely calm.
>
> The men were amazed and asked, "What kind of man is this? Even the winds and the waves obey him!" —Matthew 8:23–27

In this passage Jesus confronts a spirit, Furious, that is operating through a *sudden* onsetting storm. It's my belief this is a high-level spirit that ruled over the region of Galilee for years. It's hell-bent on killing Jesus in order to retake the territory the spirit lost due to Christ's teaching and healing ministry in the area.

But Jesus is unafraid when he is awakened by his panicked disciples. After all, his purpose on this earth has yet to be fulfilled. Why should he fear? This same concept applies to us. Why should we fear when we know God's purposes in our lives are yet to be fulfilled. God desires a long, productive life for his children. This concept is repeated throughout the Bible. So, if you are breathing, you have a purpose. Fear not!

Jesus arose and rebuked, or commanded with his voice, the demonic storm to calm down. And immediately—I mean immediately—the winds and waves subsided. The spirit in the storm was compelled to obey. We confidently assume the armies of heaven and the Holy Spirit stood ready and participated in binding this territorial spirit and destroying its evil intents.

This is our example. We speak or rebuke the storm we face, telling it to calm the heck down. In this excerpt Jesus also addresses another significant issue at hand: the disciples' fear and lack of faith. Remember it's our faith stance that empowers our badge and weapon. We stand in confident expectation instead of fear.

In the end the disciples were saved. They responded with awe and praise. This is our same response. We are saved, delivered, healed, and we stand in awe. We offer praise and thanksgiving. Neat!

But how do we arrive in a situation that requires our badge and weapon in the first place?

College Buddies?

Let's imagine an old college buddy who nearly flunked out of school for drinking too much. You and your spouse retain a distant friendship as you share a few common memories from the good ole days.

Well, one day this friend shows up while you were at the market; he moves in with his dirty duffel bag into the back bedroom. You are surprised and puzzled, wondering how he arrived at your house and found his way inside. However, you shrug off the check in your gut because you remember he's kind of fun. Or at least he used to be when you were wild and far away from God. And you think to yourself, *No big deal. My husband must have let him in. It will be fine.*

But the next time you see this guy, he's holding a twelve-pack and your husband is drinking along. Pizza boxes are all over the coffee table, and the kids aren't ready for bed. The house is an absolute wreck. Arriving home from Bible study, the peaceful spirit you carry disappears, replaced by rising anger as you survey the disaster before you. You stare at this distant college friend, who was only staying for a couple of days in the back bedroom. Now it's apparent he's moved into the living room where the TV is blazing with perversion and your family has absolutely gone wild.

How did this happen?

An open door.

And on top of that, your family isn't armored in a strong faith and they lack spiritual discernment. It's difficult to take ground back once the party is in full swing in the living room. And conflict with our spouse and children becomes inevitable. Out of necessity, we are the killjoy. Our spouse doesn't perceive that this guy is the temptation that will destroy his mind with alcohol, ruin his job, and hurt his marriage and family. Hubby believes it's just all fun and games. And *that* is the deception (Romans 8:7).

In actuality our husbands are typically great men; they are good providers and good dads. But in moments of weakness, the demonic gain entry through crafty and well-hidden or unknown open doors when a person is unaware or weakened emotionally or physically or, worse, intentionally partnering with evil. Evil entities continually press, tempt, and lie in an attempt to discover an access point. Once access is established, their covert mission is to slowly create bondage and oppress the family.

The open door in this scenario is the old friendship with the world. We missed the subtle signs because of its familiarity and failed to kick it out early on. Adding to the challenge is hubby doesn't believe there is evil behind this "old friend."

However—and praise God, there is always a *however* with Jesus— we have spiritual perception as well as wisdom. My friend, when an ordinary believer who rises early in the morning to spend time with Jesus and prays protection and the attributes of heaven over himself or herself, their mate, and their home, it's an entirely different story.

The guy (demon) from our college years won't even come a knockin'. Open doors that allow entry to unwanted squatters are shut tight and locked down. We release peace and goodness through blessing into our home. That is an atmosphere that freaks the demons out, and they hesitate to tangle with a Holy Spirit–filled, spitfire believer.

Enforcers and Open Doors

An oppressor opens doors through a number of engineered or advantageous opportunities:

- Fearful and vulnerable circumstances
- Ignorance of the spiritual realm
- Occult involvement

- Prenatal influences, such as fear, rejection, and generational curses
- Soulish domination and manipulation by another person
- Early childhood pressures, such as strife with parents and/or in the home, school challenges, sexual trauma
- Moments of emotional or physical weakness or trauma
- Sinful acts or habits *Derek Prince Ministries

For many believers the devils will try to wear us down through over-work, busyness, and conflict. And in moments when we are especially weary, Satan slams us with a traumatic event such as an unexpected death of a close relative, job loss, relational upheaval, etc. This is a moment of physical *and* emotional weakness. The enemy attempts to introduce a spirit of depression, hopelessness, and even a spirit of death or suicide.

If we are weak in our faith life, feeling far away from the Lord, over-whelmed by the unexpected and our never-ending to-do lists, we might start to feel then agree with depressive and hopeless thoughts. This is why nurturing a daily relationship with the Lord is essential. Although an attempt to access the soul realm is made, the evil one is denied hospi-tality because we remain Jesus focused. We bounce back from trauma and weakness; therefore, the demonic cannot abide.

The demonic searches for encroachment prospects. However, that's when as kingdom enforcers we step with our badge confidently in place, our enforcement weapon ready, and we speak with a firm voice. We command those marauders out, in the name of Jesus, and engage the power of the Holy Spirit. We blast them from the premises with our faith and enforcement.

The demons are doomed. They see a maturing child of God, a holy firecracker, coming at them with a golden badge, ablaze in glory, and they start to freak out. They try to hide. They will lie, then deceive because they know they are no match for a true enforcer of God's realm. The demons understand we are armed and ready to dispatch them back to the pit from whence they came. And this truth frightens the crap out of them.

One more thing that wisdom offers us as believers is to be diligent to protect our time. We must carefully choose how we give away our time, not overcommitting. God will prune things from our life, but it's wisdom not to take too much on in the first place. Self-care is God's care. We can't fight for others if we are weary and overwhelmed. Take time to reevaluate your commitments, and keep your schedule free with enough margin for the unexpected.

Open Doors of the Unequally Yoked

Over the years I've become familiar with most of the common open doors in a spiritually mismatched marriage. I will affirm it is incredibly frustrating and challenging to fight these same demons over and over again that show up in our lives. Our own repetitive sin cycles open doors. And also, the sin cycles of our spouse such as pornography, evil television, movies, and music, alcoholism, mental illness, narcissistic behaviors, etc. are open doors that we must shut. And shut. And shut again and again. Grrrrrr. However, we must shut them. And we will shut them because we know the truth and we have the ability.

Remain relentless to cast evil from your home and family. The devils eventually grow weary and give up. They will look elsewhere for unsuspecting victims. Revisits from past sin issues will be brought forward from time to time, as evil returns to check for any tiny crack in the door. It is part of your armament to remain steadfast in your faith stance against evil.

This also requires establishing effective boundaries with your spouse, children, and any other adults who live in your home. Pray and ask the Lord to identify and establish absolutes in your life. Absolutes should be few but have strong consequences with follow-through. Every healthy relationship is built upon healthy boundaries. Seek help from a Christian counselor to establish foundational boundaries and good communication with your spouse if you struggle in this area. Read books and study, even if your spouse refuses to study along with you. You do the work and allow the Lord to partner with you.

The Power of God

You are on a holy mission, redeeming hearts, souls, homes, and entire family lines through the name of Jesus. This is how we engage our power and authority for our family members who are unaware of the King or who are in rebellion against his truth.

The day I spoke to the marauder hiding behind my husband's eyes as we argued over the desk was the first day I stood with my badge and weapon, somewhat shaky and not fully convinced evil would listen. But to my astonishment, evil had no choice but to submit. And immediately. Praise God!

Cadet, in this training manual I have accentuated the power of the Holy Spirit. We often overlook the Spirit of God who is within us. For me, I will literally call upon the Holy Spirit to come and help me when I begin to pray with someone. I say aloud, "Come, Holy Spirit."

I also want to accentuate the power of Jesus. Our Savior is the ultimate authority on earth. The Scriptures also point to his ultimate power as well. Jesus demonstrates God's given power as *Dunamis*, which translated from the Greek means inherent force, strength, or ability to accomplish supernatural miracles. It is the root word of our English words *dynamite*, *dynamo*, and *dynamic*.

In Mark 5, we read about God's divine (Dunamis) power, in particular, the Holy Spirit's power at work through Jesus. In this passage the Lord frees a demon-possessed man (Mark 5:6–8). Then he raises a twelve-year-old girl back to life through the same power (Mark 5:40–42).

This is the same power within us. As Jesus said,

> You will receive power when the Holy Spirit comes on you; *and you will be my witnesses in Jerusalem, and in all Judea and Samaria, and to the ends of the earth. —Acts 1:8 (emphasis mine)*

Cadet, we are equipped with power and authority. We have the ability and an inherent force to participate in the miraculous and decimate evil. It's simply time to believe it. So let's wear our badge proudly and always have our show of force readied. And finally, practice often. Begin with some of these suggestions.

Is anger a constant in your home? Try taking authority over it every day, out loud, during your prayer time and casting it out. Then always follow your command with a blessing. Bless your home with peace, unity, love, gentleness, and self-control.

In the name of Jesus, I stand in the authority, Christ. I bind (Matthew 16:19) every lying spirit and all spirits of deception and the spirit of anger and rage. Right now! I command you to leave my home, myself, my spouse [by name] and children [each by name]. I repent on behalf of myself, my husband, and my children for any way we have partnered with anger. Now I break all legal rights with the demonic realm. I command you to get out now and never return. And as you go, take sarcasm, pride, and ignorance with you. There can be no retaliation or replacement spirits. In Jesus's name, amen!

The power of blessing is lifechanging. Practice praying and speaking this: *I bless my home with the shalom of heaven and with authentic joy. In Jesus's name, amen.*

This is another powerful blessing for difficult relationships: *I bless my relationship with my husband* [sister, mother, friend, etc.] *with a spirit of unity and cooperation, love, honor, and respect. In the name of Jesus Christ.* I speak this blessing over every difficult relationship consistently until there is change. I prayed for almost a year over a twenty-year broken sibling relationship. When God began to move, this relationship was restored within a matter of months. Jesus rocks!

Practice: Do you deal with silent treatment? Try this prayer:

Father, right now, in the name of Jesus I command this spirit of punishment, shaming, and bitterness to be banished from my home. I command it out of my spouse and out of our relationship dynamic. I declare today that our marriage is a place of trust, love, and safety. I declare that the spirit of fear, the spirit or need to punish and ignore, is defeated by the blood of Jesus.

Right now I break the silence as I declare Jesus was broken for restoration, including our relationship and marriage. I release love, kindness, gentleness, and healthy communication in love between my spouse and me. I bless our relationship with trust. I bless us to speak words of love, encouragement, and hope to one another. In the mighty name of Jesus, amen!

Follow-up suggestion: Take communion daily as you pray over relational conflicts. Invite the power of the body and blood of Jesus into your life and prayer.

Jesus and the Holy Spirit

Partnering with the Holy Spirit is essential. Did you know that the supernatural ministry of Jesus began following his baptism in the Jordan? Take a look.

Then Jesus came from Galilee to the Jordan to be baptized by John. But John tried to deter him, saying, "I need to be baptized by you, and do you come to me?"

Jesus replied, "Let it be so now; it is proper for us to do this to fulfill all righteousness." Then John consented.

As soon as Jesus was baptized, he went up out of the water. At that moment heaven was opened, and he saw the Spirit of God *descending* like a dove and alighting on him. *And a voice from heaven said, "This is my Son, whom I love; with him I am well pleased." —Matthew 3:13–17 (emphasis mine)*

In the chapter following this passage, we read that Jesus was tested by the devil for forty days and nights. After his temptation, Jesus and his disciples attended a wedding in Cana. That is where Jesus turned water into wine, his first supernatural miracle (John 2:1–11).

Jesus became filled with the power of the Holy Spirit. Miracles ensued, and people were healed from that moment forward. The lame walked. The deaf heard, and those afflicted by the devil were set free.

This is our mandate, church. Walk in the authority of Christ, partnering with the power of the Holy Spirit.

I'll share it again because Jesus is our ultimate example of what is possible when we walk in his authority and in the power of the Holy Spirit:

Heal the sick, raise the dead, cleanse those who have leprosy, drive out demons. Freely you have received; freely give. —Matthew 10:8

Congratulations! Cadet, you have acquired your stance. We now stand in our authority and with the power of Christ and the Holy Spirit through our identity as children of God and our relational intimacy with the Father. I hope the next time you study Ephesians 6:10–11 you perceive and understand the great wealth and depths of an ordinary believer who stands in faith.

You have passed this part of academy training! You are empowered to bring God's kingdom to earth as it is in heaven! Hallelujah!

Ephesians 6
Take up the shield of faith, with which you can extinguish all the flaming arrows of the evil one.

Chapter Six
REALMS OF JURISDICTION

Therefore I also, after I heard of your faith in the Lord Jesus and your love for all the saints, do not cease to give thanks for you, making mention of you in my prayers: that the God of our Lord Jesus Christ, the Father of glory, may give to you the spirit of wisdom and revelation in the knowledge of Him, the eyes of your understanding being enlightened; that you may know what is the hope of His calling, what are the riches of the glory of His inheritance in the saints, and what is the exceeding greatness of His power toward us who believe, according to the working of His mighty power which He worked in Christ when He raised Him from the dead and seated Him at His right hand in the heavenly places, far above all principality and power and might and dominion, and every name that is named, not only in this age but also in that which is to come. *And He put all things under His feet, and gave Him to be head over all things to the church, which is His body, the fullness of Him who fills all in all.*
—Ephesians 1:15–23 (NKJV, emphasis mine)

Enforcement Officer's Jurisdiction: Self

The powerful place from which we fight is our stance. Now it's time to understand how we defend our jurisdiction.

As spouses who are married to unbelievers, defining where and when we have the ability and opportunity to affect change in our life is crucial. The training I've shared thus far equips us with power and authority from on high that we may bring the supernatural power of God into our circumstances.

Through years of Bible study application and engagement in day-to-day warfare, I define areas under my spiritual influence as my jurisdiction. These "arcas" are mine to defend and advance for the kingdom of Jesus Christ. My jurisdiction will shift, grow, expand, or contract depending on various factors. However, there exist defined areas of jurisdiction that consistently come under my influence. And I'm mandated to protect them through faith and prayer.

Our primary jurisdiction begins with self. We have the highest authority over ourselves because we exercise our free will. This personal jurisdiction includes our mind, intellect, will, choice, and emotions (the soul realm) as well as our physical body. I cover these areas of my person consistently with prayer, aligning myself to the will and purposes of God. I also ask the Lord to reveal any lies I've entertained in my thought life as well as to reveal my emotional state and feelings or errors in exercising my free will. I then pray and command my will, thoughts, and emotions to align with the truth of the Bible and with his purposes for my day. I bless myself with a sound mind and strength of character.

I also command any illness or even the fears of contracting an illness or affliction to leave me immediately. I then lay my own hands on any area of my body that is ill or where I feel pain or even tenderness, and I bless it with healing in Jesus's name. Remember, always bless in the name of Jesus. I assign angels of healing to lay hands on me and administer the healing of Jesus over my body.

Nearly every day, I bless myself with divine health. In Jesus's name.

Enforcement Officer's Jurisdiction: Outside Self

The expansion of our jurisdiction outside ourselves is predicated on a variety of factors. But overall, there are three areas that consistently fall under our ability to influence through prayer. These areas are what we love, what we steward, and everything under our responsibility, awareness, and service. This is our expanded jurisdiction.

Over time, it becomes easier to define and then expand areas we desire to influence for the kingdom of God. For example, I love my family. My prayers are powerful for my children, and several scriptures back up this truth. I am also in covenant with my husband. Our marriage is a covenant of love and sanctioned by God's kingdom as a blood covenant. This covenant is recognized in the unseen realm and provides me with a respected ability to exert great influence over our marriage and to defeat evil. And I am able to battle confidently through belief and faith for the benefit of my husband and my family relationships and for our home in general.

Because we are children of God, our physical home is an area where we possess tremendous influence. Other areas of influence include our workplace, church, ministry as well as places we visit regularly, such as the grocery store, the bank, and the post office.

We carry the living God within us. He desires peace, joy, and righteousness for all of humanity (Romans 14:17). God is excited and thrilled when we take his authority into the world and release his supernatural presence, healing, deliverance, and love.

What does this look like in everyday life?

Well, the example of praying for the woman who passed out at the woman's luncheon is certainly an example of carrying God's authority and power. Another absolutely fun example is strolling the produce aisle at the grocery store with the Holy Spirit. It's a blast to release God's blessings and love among the shoppers. Some of the passersby hear my blessing, and some don't. But it's so much fun to watch their faces change, their frustration depart, and a smile appear as the Lord releases his love and heavenly atmosphere into the store.

More recently, in various conversations, the Holy Spirit has prompted me to ask a person, "Have you prayed the prayer of salvation?" Just this past week I asked this question of my realtor. We were speaking about Jesus as a healer. Regularly now, I have led people through a prayer of faith. I simply ask them to repeat after me. And they accept Jesus as their Lord and Savior. Then the most astonishing thing happens. The Holy Spirit floods the room, and they have an encounter with the love and reality of God. This usually creates tears of joy, for both of us. What a privilege to be a daughter of God.

I once released God's presence when there was bickering, fighting, and mischief happening in line at Wal-Mart. I also bless nearly every person who steps into our house. I've been told that our home is a place of peace. It's the presence of the Holy Spirit. This is everyday life.

This is the good life!

I consistently remain armored in my stance at some level of awareness. I have a watchful eye, and I'm ready to defeat any demonic infiltrator that might try to steal from me, my spouse, or my home.

Again, I'll point out that we stand in our authority when we are aligned with the character and purposes of God (righteousness). *Our authority is never a weapon of control.* We cannot subvert the free will of an individual.

The best way to partner with Jesus and the Holy Spirit is to emulate the examples of Christ and the early church believers found in the New Testament.

Then Jesus went about all the cities and villages, teaching in their synagogues, preaching the gospel of the kingdom, and healing every sickness and every disease among the people. But when He saw the multitudes, He was moved with compassion for them, because they were weary and scattered, like sheep having no shepherd. —Matthew 9:35–36 (NKJV)

The compassion of Jesus precipitated his miraculous healings. His love for people who were suffering under terrible afflictions motivated his deliverance ministry. Led by the Spirit, he spoke truth, unlocking the downtrodden from the invisible chains of bondage.

Our jurisdiction is a mission of love and compassion. Our jurisdiction is governed well when we love with a heart like Christ. Love—it's the most powerful force on earth.

Do you want to influence your spouse? Love. What about your children's friends? Love. How about your city? Ask the Lord to reveal how to love your city well. Love is something the devils cannot abide. They only know hate. Love defeats hate. Absolutely.

And now these three remain: faith, hope and love. But the greatest of these is love. —1 Corinthians 13:13

Jurisdiction Prayer

The usual start to my day is placing my badge on my chest. Well, actually, I really never take it off. I've experienced some pretty intense skirmishes during the nighttime hours. Yep, I've battled a few doozies at 3:00 a.m. Sheesh!

I pray a jurisdiction prayer, something like this:

Father, in the name of Jesus, I take this moment to establish a perimeter of protection, a dome of light, love, and the blood of Jesus over my home and land, my family, my marriage, and everything under my roof. Place your protection within and around my home [around my workplace, etc.]. I forbid any evil spirits from having a voice or any influence in my home [office, workplace, etc.]. I cover any open door or portal with the blood of Jesus. Father, close every area of access now. Please cleanse all sin or evil from our home and all who live within. Please protect my spouse, children, animals, cars, and my person from all illness and accidents. Bless each of us with divine health and divine provision. In Jesus's name.

Father, I also ask that you place under your protection our possessions, our home, bank accounts, investments, ministry, and all those who serve in ministry under my name. Father, I forbid any evil advancements into any area that is under my love, stewardship, or jurisdiction. In the mighty name of Jesus.

Father, please bless every area of my responsibility and service. Bless my body and mind. Bless my will and emotions. Prosper all that I put my mind and hands toward today. Thank you for your goodness toward me. Thank you for your faithfulness and your love that overwhelms me. Pour out greater revelation of your love over me, my spouse, my kids, and my ministry. In Jesus's name, I pray. Amen.

I recall that within the first few months of living in our new home, we experienced numerous breakages in our house. The spa failed, the pool backed up, and it was one thing after another that required fixing and money we didn't have. When I finally realized what was happening, I took authority over any devil that was on assignment to break, destroy, or cause failure in our home. I commanded it out, *now!* In Jesus's name.

That night as we were sleeping, a glass shelf fell in the dining area. I jumped from bed and found that only a single plate was broken. But as I stood there, I sensed that the enemy was finally defeated. I could feel it in my soul that this was the last afront because the demon was forced to leave. I truly sensed it leave in a huff out the front door, breaking the plate in its rush. Wild!

And sure enough, after that, no further breakages occurred in or around our home. Hallelujah! Commanding prayer works!

Practice by establishing a perimeter. Pray aloud asking for cleansing and protection over yourself, your home, and your family. Then establish perimeter boundaries over all that you love and steward and everything under your jurisdiction. Always release blessings and promises of God. In Jesus's name, amen.

Remember, our greatest weapon is our stance. Our stance is persistence. We persist in unwavering belief in the Word of God, knowing it is truth and it works. We remain steadfast in pursuit of the promises, teaching, and examples of Christ. Our life and character are established upon this rock, a persistent and steadfast faith.

Stance = persistent faith. Amen!

Spiritual Enforcer

Ephesians 6

Take up the shield of
faith, with which you
can extinguish all the
flaming arrows of the
evil one.

Part Two

Works of Darkness

For we do not wrestle against flesh and blood, but against principalities, against powers, against the rulers of the darkness of this age, against spiritual hosts of wickedness in the heavenly places. —Ephesians 6:12 (NKJV)

Chapter Seven
LIARS, SABOTEURS, AND COVERT OPERATIONS

But if I cast out demons with the finger of God, surely the kingdom of God has come upon you. —Luke 11:20 (NKJV)

Defeating the Demonic Realm

Cadet, so far in our training we have gained our powerful stance and have readied ourselves for the fight. But who are we really fighting and defending against? It's not our spouse. It's not the government. It's not the culture. Ephesians 6 defines our adversaries as principalities, powers, rulers, and spiritual hosts of wickedness in the heavenly places.

As we peer into the unseen realm, let's remember we are not demon focused. Our eyes remain fixed on Jesus, the author and perfector of our faith. Nor is this study a matter of salvation or the sovereignty and love of our Father. It's merely an area of the realm that influences our daily lives. Therefore, we must be made aware and become equipped. As we move forward, we are resolved to this truth:

The God of peace will soon crush Satan under your feet. The grace of our Lord Jesus be with you. AMEN —Romans 16:20

Before we begin, I sense urging from the Lord that we remain in faith and do not fear the evil realm. Satan's main weapon is fear, but we defeat fear through faith and love. Mystery and misunderstanding abound regarding the evil realm. This is quite intentional. The devil and his minions are diligent to remain hidden in the shadows, undetected. Covert attacks prove highly successful.

Let's get started. A recent Gallup Poll surveyed American adults and reported that 74 percent of survey responders said they believe in God. Interestingly, 58 percent of these same responders reported that they did not believe in hell or Satan.[1]

Satan likes to disappear. *There's nothing here, folks.* That's his favorite ruse. Therefore, a great number of people, including churchgoers, are vulnerable and oppressed because of their ignorance. The predominant belief in Western culture, including a large portion of the Christian church, is that demons are nothing more than a figment of one's imagination.

It grieves me to know many clergy, Bible teachers, and pastors remain unaware and unprepared to defend their congregants against evil or instruct believers in deliverance or the effects of demonic oppression.

Because there is a lack in some church leadership in this area, I'm compelled to shed some light into this realm. When you shine the light of God into darkness, do you know what happens? It loses power!

The Bible attests to the very real existence of Satan and demons. In order to enforce your authority in Christ over evil, it's essential that we uncloak the demonic realm, thereby removing the mystery and fear.

Let's begin with an irrefutable truth. Our Father, Yahweh, created the heavens and the earth. His dominion is absolute. He assigned humanity to rule and reign, to have dominion, over the earth. This privilege was lost with the fall of Adam and Eve.

Jesus, the son of God, atoned for the fall of humanity and, through his sacrifice, took back the keys of ultimate authority from Satan. He passed his authority to his disciples, his church, to enforce and bring God's kingdom to earth as it is in heaven. We reviewed these truths in the first section of this book. Most of the supernatural ministry of Jesus was teaching these precepts and offering us living examples of how we exert our authority as his followers.

God's kingdom reigns. However, Satan usurps God's intents and purposes through the hijacking of individuals' free will. Satan deceives humanity and convinces people to willfully believe his lies in order to advance his agenda on earth.

What is his primary purpose? Jesus reveals the purpose of his evil ministry and immediately contrasts that with his purpose and ministry in a single statement:

> *The thief comes only to steal and kill and destroy; I have come that they may have life, and have it to the full. —John 10:10*

The Bible states that Satan is the head of the demonic realm and the father of all lies.

> *The great dragon was hurled down—that ancient serpent called the devil, or Satan, who leads the whole world astray. He was hurled to the earth, and his angels with him. —Revelation 12:9*

Jesus said: *You belong to your father, the devil, and you want to carry out your father's desires. He was a murderer from the beginning, not holding to the truth, for there is no truth in him. When he lies, he speaks his native language, for he is a liar and the father of lies. —John 8:44*

In addition to deceiving humans into evil service, Satan enslaved a hierarchy of evil beings to assist in his diabolical diatribe which has existed for millennia.

> *For we do not wrestle against flesh and blood, but against principalities, against powers, against the rulers of the darkness of this age, against spiritual hosts of wickedness in the heavenly places. —Ephesians 6:12 (NKJV)*

Hierarchy

Let's review this hierarchy Paul teaches in Ephesians 6:12. I offer the descriptions below from my research and review of commentaries from well-known and trusted biblical theologians, as translated from the Greek text of the New Testament.

Satan: commander-in-chief
Principalities: ancient ones, princes
Powers: authorities, delegated powers
Rulers of darkness of this world: Emperors of darkness, regional spirits, a trained order, order of raw power
Spiritual wickedness: wicked spirits, bad, vile, malevolent, vicious, immoral, and malicious in high places (heavenly places, realm between earth and God's domain)

The dark kingdom is definitively structured and highly organized. Complete obedience is marshalled through pain, intimidation, fear, and hate. This crushing power structure is administered from the very top through the overlords, down through the rank and file, to underlings.

When researching the demonic realm, there exist several differing opinions in Christian theology and belief as to the origin of demons. In my examination, their origin is inconclusive. We won't explore those suppositions in this book, but they are interesting to investigate.

Low-Level Demons

For most of us, our skirmishes are primarily with wicked spirits or earth-bound demons. Through my personal study and years of deliverance experience, I describe a common demon as a disembodied spirit. They are sentient beings with a will and personality. They crave a habitation of longevity, primarily a human physical body or an animal; they will also attach to objects, with an intention to live out their desires and perverted assignments. They never tire in their endeavors to manipulate people through sin, distortion, deception, and lies. They feed on human and animal pain and misery.

These surface-level beings work to oppress, inhabit, and create pain. The endgame is to grow pride and rebellion or create death through continual defeat, in the heart of individual, thus turning a person away from God. They are spirits of affliction, infirmity, addiction, pain, trauma, lust, religious spirits, witchcraft, every form of perversion, and many others, too numerous to name. They look for any open door in a person's soul in which to gain entry in an effort to manifest confusion and deception. Once they gain entry, they oppress and torment. They will not leave willingly.

There are many of these spirits that are assigned to families. They travel through the generations and possess tremendous knowledge regarding the failings and sins of our ancestors. These familiar spirits perpetuate the same sins, increasing the sin's stronghold and influence, generation upon generation. This is the ongoing demonic activity that many of us deal with in our lives. Demonic oppression is commonly observed in multiple generations with recurring sins, addictions, and hang-ups such as alcoholism, depression, premature death, infidelity, premarital pregnancy, and infertility as a few examples.

As far back as I'm able to research, I discovered several of these strongholds in every generation of my own family. Ack!

I believe the church struggles with confusion and fear in this area of demonic activity, oppression, and possession. In my experience, possession is ownership. However, Christians are owned by the Holy Spirit. They are not possessed by evil unless they have invited it in and turned away from Christ. However, demons do not hesitate to take advantage of legal rights and our ignorance. With every opportunity possible, they initiate oppression, striving to dwell around or within a believer. Oppression is the ongoing torment of an individual. Oppression is easily identified when we hold up the issue, circumstance, or difficulty to the truth in the Word of God. For example, consider fear. Scripture is filled with passages that teach believers to fear not.

And of course, it's common to experience demonic activity around us or in and around others.

I'll state it again, it's crucial to reject sin, work through trauma, and diligently pursue obedience as a believer. The greater our alignment to the Word of God, the less we experience oppression and visitation from demonic spirits.

The majority of our battles are with these surface-level entities.

Higher Levels of Evil

On occasion we may find ourselves in conflict with a higher level of evil, principalities, or territorial spirits. For example, a few years ago, I joined two of my prayer partners at the kitchen table. I can't recall the exact reason we met for prayer. However, I recall with sharp focus what happened when we began to pray in an unauthorized area.

We each took turns praying, and after about twenty minutes, our prayers turned away from our initial focus. Without asking the Lord for direction, we turned our prayers to confront a five-star casino and some shady dealings related to the place. This property is operated by Mission Indians and has existed near the mountain ridge at the south end of the valley where we lived for hundreds of years. As we began to pray against the area and against the addictions of gaming, searing pain suddenly pierced my head. I was hit with a five-star migraine. Headaches are rare for me, and over the years I've learned when I experience a migraine while in prayer, it's the result of witchcraft.

I start yelling with increasing volume, "My head. My head." And the ladies rushed to pray for me. Fairly quickly the pain subsided. It was a bizarre and very confusing prayer session, to say the least. We continued to pray a little longer regarding another area of concern, but we left the casino alone. We concluded our prayer time, and I headed home.

The next morning, I awoke still very confused about the migraine attack of the previous day. I went to the Father in prayer and asked him, *Lord, what happened yesterday when we were praying?*

He replied, *Lynn, did I tell you to go after that thing?*

No, Lord. You didn't.

Then in my mind the Lord revealed a picture of this giant, dark, wicked being, who stood twenty stories tall, leaning back against the hillside watching the valley floor and the casino. It was the principality spirit that rules and oversees the casino domain. As I watched this vision unfold, there appeared black, oily streams flowing into and out of the casino. These were streams of iniquity such as gambling, prostitution, addiction, trafficking, and a number of other seedy activities of the underworld.

But Lord, why was I attacked when we prayed against this thing?

And the Father patiently replied, *It's protected by witchcraft. They— the people of the domain—worship the tree at the center of the land. They reverence it and believe it holds power. You don't have the right to come against it because of this worship. They want it there.*

Yowzah! A lesson learned the hard way. There are higher powers, principalities, and rulers that exceed our faith or authority to challenge. Our prayer team did not have a legal right to come against this stronghold in the valley because it was worshiped by the people. The principality has a legal right to remain.

Even so, situations and opportunities will arise when these larger areas of dominion should be challenged, but only after prayer and certainty that God is with you. Let me share an example.

In the fall of 2018, after years of drought conditions in California, I was praying for rain, and the Lord revealed a throne to me during my prayer time. While praying, I could see in my mind a throne floating in the air above the city of Los Angeles. I perceived this was the authority that was diverting the rainstorms that normally flow down the coast from the north. The storms veered away from the south and were pushed off to the northeast, thereby missing Southern California completely.

As I continued to pray, I suddenly saw myself cloaked in a royal robe holding a scepter in my hand. Instinctively, I knew what I should do. In my prayer vision, I approached this throne and some evil thing slithered off and disappeared. This territorial spirit immediately recognized my authority and abandoned this throne of authority.

I sat down on the throne and began to prophesy rain. Aloud I spoke until out of breath, "Bring storm, after storm, after storm, after storm, after storm . . ." In early February, the rain-laden clouds arrived. The successive winter storms didn't stop until June. The drought ended in a glorious super bloom of wildflowers and billions of butterflies that year!

That was a miracle. Somehow, through my petitions, I became authorized to pray against that ruler who sat on that throne of power. Also, I asked the Lord to fill that seat of power with an angelic ruler to oversee the normal flow of rain. I also know many of God's people were praying in accord with my petitions. I love how the kingdom works that way. Did I do this alone? Likely no. But it was wild to partner with God in this adventure.

These two examples again are reflective of our intimate relationship with God. Because I hadn't asked God about the casino, I experienced pushback in the form of witchcraft. In contrast, I was prayerfully seeking God's mercy and rain. This prayer was honored, as rain is always a blessing from his hand. Intimacy created my knowing of his character and goodness toward the earth and humanity.

As we mature in faith, we unlock greater access to defeat evil. However, we continually pray and battle to enforce God's kingdom in the areas we already oversee. Our jurisdictions will expand as we mature, love, pray, and ask for more.

Legal Rights

We have reviewed some of the rank and file of the evil realm. The most important thing to know about the demonic realm is they cannot do anything without a legal right. And we have the power and authority to deny the legal rights of the enemy in the territories God has set up for us. Hallelujah!

The kingdom of God is a realm of rules, regulations, and laws. God established the spiritual and physical laws that govern our universe at creation. I'll share more about the legalities of the kingdom of God in the next chapter. It's good stuff. Stay tuned.

But for now, let's determine how an agent of evil obtains a legal right that grants access to a person. The easiest way to convey this aspect of the unseen realm is to consider the most common and primary access point of evil.

Fear

This is the weapon of choice for evil. The demonic works to create fear in our lives to the point we believe and then embrace the fear. When we willingly turn away from God and his goodness and choose fear over faith, a door of opportunity opens to the demonic, thereby allowing oppression. Once activity is established, the demonic perpetuates their work of fear. It is usually the gatekeeper who will hold the door open for more demons, adding a variant of oppression, such as depression, rage, or bitterness, thereby creating greater strongholds in an individual's life. Evil's endgame for each life on earth is ultimately that a person becomes heavily beset and hopeless, so much so, they eventually will kill others or kill themselves or both.

Yep, just typing this description makes me furious with evil.

The Bible is replete with passages that come against fear. God is fully aware that evil perpetuates fear. This is why Scripture continually teaches us to fear not.

How do we defeat fear?

Through belief and confidence in Jesus Christ and the assurances that he is with us, protecting, leading, and loving us. Fear is defeated when we stand in convicted faith, believing the Bible over our impossible circumstances even when they appear scary or even downright terrifying.

It's always about choice. What will our free will choose? Do we choose to believe fear, or do we choose truth? When we partner with truth, the oppressor is defeated. Remember in chapter 3, we learned these very important declarations of faith: *I will not partner with fear. I will not partner with doubt.*

Therefore submit to God. Resist the devil and he will flee from you. —
James 4:7 (NKJV)

Resistance defeats evil every time. Choose rightly and STAND!

Trauma Wounds

Trauma is another way the demons introduce lies and deception that open the door to oppression. The devil does not play fair. His efforts to destroy us begin at a very young age.

For example, an innocent child is born into a loving family, which is not always the case for many of us. However, let's continue with this young girl's story. She feels and experiences love from her parents. As she grows into her toddler years, she feels loved, safe, wanted, and good. However, the demonic realm's main mission is to kill, steal, or destroy this child, thereby leaving her ineffectual to love and serve God. Satan is aware if he's able to hurt enough, he creates an opportunity to steal her true identity and prohibit the fulfillment of her earthly missions, her destiny.

The devil introduces trauma.

The human soul was never made to endure trauma. The effects of trauma are deep, with some trauma wounds imparting pain and lies that last a lifetime.

Recently, I was working through a prayer session with a woman who was revisiting the trauma that introduced fear, abandonment, and rejection into her life. She is the young child in this example. Her trauma began while camping with her aunt and uncle. At age five or six, she became separated from her family and wandered for hours, lost in the woods.

Eventually, an officer found her and reunited her with her aunt and uncle. However, the damage was done. As she wandered the woods, terror gripped her. She began to listen to the voice of fear, abandonment, and insignificance. She believed this lying voice and forged an invisible but very real "legal" agreement, or bond, with the spirit of fear and abandonment. She no longer believed she was safe, loved, or protected. She no longer believed God was good. Her true identity was stolen away from her.

The trauma and false identity opened a door allowing the liar to cohabitate and oppress her. Unknowingly, she legally moved her allegiance, her free will, from the truth, love, and care of God to false gods, or demon oppressors. In this case, the spirt of fear and the orphan spirit.

Because she never processed this trauma through the love and healing truth of Jesus, this lie remained embedded in her soul throughout her adulthood. Well, that was until Jesus revealed that she wasn't abandoned and he had always been with her. And then Jesus healed the trauma wound and set her free from crippling fear of abandonment. She was forty years old.

When Jesus healed the trauma and exposed the lie, she stepped out of oppression, depression, and the fear of abandonment and moved into truth and life. The healing experience created within her a greater love bond with Jesus.

She lived nearly forty years with a false narrative. It grieves me, and it grieves Jesus.

Unfortunately, lies and the accompanying oppression begin early. The demonic will do everything in its power to extend and calcify fear and rejection into a person's identity. He uses our relationships with others, exerting control over those with whom demons have great influence, as well as difficult circumstances to punctuate the primary lie repeatedly throughout the years. The result is a trauma bond with a lie and false identity and a lot of unnecessary suffering and pain.

We know from Scripture that when evil gains a foothold, it invites seven other spirits more wicked than itself (Matthew 12:45). This malice is secretive and, of course, destructive. I've found that few believers truly understand the unseen realm and the ultimate endgame of their sworn enemy: our utter destruction.

We are bound by a legal kingdom. When we live and operate from the truths and principles of God's Word, we are free. We are not held captive to an orphan spirit. We are free from the manipulation of fear and depression. We have a hope and a future. We are prosperous and live a very satisfying and good life.

As I said in the first section of the book, lies, deceptions, and distortions are the inroads to legal activity that benefits the demonic realm. Our responsibility is to unwind the lies, align with truth, and then command evil out. We possess the power and authority to free ourselves and then to help others become free. It's not scary. It's not difficult. It's merely believing and then doing the work.

One more thought: when we align with the Word and live from its premise, we are in a legal agreement with the Lord. We are legally bound to God and offered his promises, which are numerous and life-giving.

I hope this explanation brings light and hope. Jesus is the healer of every trauma. He is the way, the truth, and the life. Freedom is our promise! The kingdom of God is at hand.

And as you go, preach, saying, "The kingdom of heaven is at hand." — *Matthew 10:7 (NKJV) (emphasis mine)*

Prepared for Enforcement

The best prayer work I ever engaged in for myself was asking the Lord, *What lies am I believing?*

I spent several years praying, confessing, and even grieving through a lifetime of lies. I repented through the decades of personal sin. I prayed to understand the lies that held me captive, then literally *changed my mind* and chose the truth.

This prayer work finally landed me on the day where I came face-to-face with the massive lie at the core of my heart. *Is God truly good?* Interesting how this lie is cloaked in a question. This satanic operation is as old as time. He used the same question to deceive Eve in the garden.

For me, this lie was rooted in tremendous distrust of people that began when I was a child, then fortified as a young adult. I believed I couldn't trust anyone. It was a process to unwind the tangles of lies and bondage. But when I finally emerged, fully comprehending in the depth of my soul that God is absolutely good and trustworthy, my reality altered. I experienced freedom. My life changed for the better. Much better.

Fellow cadet, take time to approach Jesus with the desire to live free. He will gently reveal unbelief and pain that requires his loving touch. Ask him to reveal the lies you believe. Then allow him to love you and reveal the truth. Read the Word, journal, pray, wait upon the Lord. He is patient and kind and always ready to heal, forgive, and bless.

Working through the healing of trauma and walking into truth is paramount in order to increase our authority and power in the spiritual realm. Why? Because a free child of God is unhindered. Our unhindered stance is the irrefutable ability to effectively defeat evil when battling for our spouses, children, and a world that is overwhelmed by pain.

Revoking Legal Rights

Delving into our fears will feel scary. Indeed, it's not always easy. Enduring a protracted root canal may feel more appealing than facing down fear, trauma, and pain. Dread and avoidance arise, and we shrink. However, facing the memories of our past as well as our personal moral failures is crucial to freedom and greater authority. Do the work of inner healing. Let's start with this simple and biblical exercise. Have a pen and paper ready.

Pray Psalm 51: *Create in me a pure heart, O God, and renew a steadfast spirit within me (Psalm 51:10).*

Listen as the Lord responds. Write down what you hear. Then follow the CRRs: confession, repentance, and renouncing. These are the power tools of healing prayer ministry. This is the ministry of Jesus. His blood offers us redemption, restoration, and transformation. We apprehend the work of the cross through this prayer process.

Let me share an example. Pray aloud and journal.

Father, I approach your throne of grace this hour to receive grace and mercy. Lord, I confess I have this hidden sin, fear, circumstance _____. I confess that this has come between us. I repent for my participation in this sinful activity and my impure thoughts. Lord, now I ask in the name of Jesus, my redeemer, to forgive this sin and cleanse me of all entanglements. Lord, I break every soul bond I have with this sin and the spirit that came with it. I declare that the evil that has held me captive is now bound because of Matthew 16:19.

Father, now in the name of Jesus, I command every evil spirit that had rights, because of this sin, to my body, soul, mind, or any part of me to leave me now and never return. The spirits must take with them all works and effects, devices and weapons. This evil is forbidden to speak or cry out for help. I forbid any spirit to go to any of my family members. And I forbid any retaliation or replacement spirits.

I now receive the power of your Holy Spirit to fill this place in my life where this sin took up space. I bless myself in the name of Jesus with _____ [opposite of the sin]. I bless myself with purity, holiness, love, acceptance, worthiness, power, authority, and a sound mind. In Jesus's name I pray and I believe. Amen!

Additionally, interceding for a family member with this type of prayer is highly effective.

Healing of Trauma Prayer

Jesus, I bring before you my great desire to live wholeheartedly in faith and confidence. I ask you to reveal any memories from my past that hold unhealed trauma. Lord, identify for me what lies have entered my belief system.

LIES:

_____

_____

_____

I crush this lie with the truth. [Find scriptures that confront the lie, and speak them aloud.

TRUTH:

_____

_____

_____

Jesus, I choose to forgive_____ for what they did _____ and the emotional pain of _____ this created in my life.

Jesus, right now I ask you to touch this memory and show me how you were with me. Remove this trauma's power by your love. Reunite that part of me that is harmed, afraid, and unloved into your wholeness. I believe in the power of your healing blood. And I receive wholeness and redemption. In your power and authority and by your name, Jesus, amen.

Prayers of Power

In the name of Jesus, today I take authority over myself and my home, and I command every evil spirt to leave right now. I command anger, distortion, fear, and the spirit of lack to get out and never return. [Add anything you sense.] *Now I ask you to bless this home with peace and your abiding presence. Lord Jesus, please move in power to bring my family into a vibrant and powerful relationship with you. I bless my family with a spirit of love and cooperation, unity, honor, and respect.*

I declare this house will serve the Lord. Place your hand of favor over everything under my attention today, and bless me with your goodness, love, and prosperity, in the name of Jesus. I bless my husband/wife in his/her work. May he/she find favor from bosses, clients, and coworkers. I bless myself with the same at work. I bless my children with a sound mind and ask you to establish within them an incorruptible identity centered in love and acceptance in Christ Jesus. I bless my home to be a place of peace, rest, laughter, authenticity, and safety. In the mighty name of Jesus, amen!

A number of years ago, when I was in the middle of my search for my true identity and to really *know* God, I prayed a passage out of Ephesians 1 for months and months.

Father, God of my Lord Jesus Christ, you are the Father of glory! I ask that you give me the spirit of wisdom, that I may be wise on earth in my work, my worship, my relationships with you and others, in everything I do and speak. I also ask for the spirit of revelation that I may know you through a deep, abiding and powerful relationship. Father, open my eyes to understanding and enlighten me to the amazing truth that you have a calling on my life. Reveal my callings and teach me to walk in them now. Father, may your callings fill me with great hope and contentment. I also ask for understanding of the riches of glory because I have an inheritance here on earth and also in heaven. Reveal this to me.

Father, what is the exceeding greatness of power that is focused toward me as a believer? Reveal this working of your mighty power in my life. The same astonishing power is made available to me as the power that raised Christ from the dead. Teach me how to partner with your power. And show me how to engage this power with Christ over and far above all principality and power and might and dominion and every name that is named, not only in this age but also in that which is to come! Hallelujah! I will defeat the kingdom of darkness for the cause of Christ Jesus!

And I declare Jesus Christ is over all things and all things are under the power and dominion of his church. Amen and amen!

Cadet, if you don't know what to pray, open your Bible and pray the words aloud, straight from the pages. Pray through Psalm 23 and Psalm 91.

We, the unequally yoked, face enormous challenges within our marriages and challenges to our faith. Despite the trials, we have persevered in becoming kingdom leaders. In our desperation we have figured out how to depend on Jesus and live out of the promises of Ephesians. We have persevered through the long crushing of our worldly desires to arrive in a powerful life of love and connection with Christ. We are the chosen who are assigned to lead many into healing and hope. It's us, the outcasts, the mismatched in marriage, the unacknowledged in church, who share God's wisdom with people who are deceived. And out of our love they shall find the truth that sets them free.

And that truth is a person. He is Jesus.

---

1. Gallup.com, June 20, 2023.

Chapter Eight
CLOSE THE DOORS

But if I cast out demons by the Spirit of God, surely the kingdom of God has come upon you. —Matthew 12:28 (NKJV)

I t's time to close the doors.

Once we have established our stance and defined our parameters in the natural and spiritual realm, we discover we live under divine protection. This environment creates an atmosphere of love, harmony, and beauty. Most of the time it's peaceful. This is the life that God desires for his children.

Even so, the demonic persists to punch holes in the walls of our protective house. They are always searching for an open door. In the life of a Christian, I find a few commonalities that offer openings to demons. I'll review several now.

Media

I love to sit outside in the summer with my Bible, my journal, steaming coffee and . . . . .

$\mathcal{M}y$ cell phone.

Cue scary music.

Yep, a cell phone is a potential portal to all kinds of evil. It's also a fantastic tool when we are the master of its content.

Instead of reading my Bible while my head was clear and focused in the morning, I would look at my email, then skip over to my social media accounts, followed by the weather app, etc. By the time I put the dang phone down, my mind was completely hijacked. I turned my focus toward my to-do list instead of focusing on the Lord.

Bringing my phone into my prayer appointment became catastrophic. My time, thoughts, and attention on God was swallowed up, especially when I ventured too far into certain social media accounts. The social media prophets of doom will scare the crap out of a person, and many of these so-called prophets are Christian. Yikes!

Cadet, God deserves our first fruits. I changed my morning routine to pick up my Bible first and pray. The social media prophets will just have to wait to tell me how the world will end today (grin) until after I fill my soul and mind with truth.

Additionally, I don't think it's necessary to detail the various invitations to engage in evil that travel across devices and screens. There are literal curses and witchcraft spells that come through our televisions, gaming consoles, and phones that are cloaked as entertainment.

Discernment becomes a powerful defensive weapon.

It's important we learn to listen with our hearts and spiritually examine the content that passes through our ears and eyes. The demon of lust, for example, captivates through prime-time television programs, where temptation is aroused subtly within the subconscious. The battle back to purity of mind becomes immense and tiring.

Every screen in our house is an open door, depending on what is streaming. I cannot overemphasize how crucial discernment becomes for ourselves and our kids. Obviously, restricting our spouse's content isn't always possible. Remember, they have free will. Yet marriage is living, compromising, and giving to one another. Discussions regarding appropriate limits and boundaries, established through mutual respect, is the course of action. Engage in an honest discussion to determine what is acceptable and respectable for you both, as well as the family. I'll add a side note: turn off the news. It's filled with hate, fear, division, and so much of it is utterly untrue. Discern how and where you obtain truth about the world, and always filter everything through the lens of God's Word.

Then pray, pray, pray, and kick evil out. We bless our homes with peace and cover it with the blood of Jesus. Ask Jesus to reveal open doors of evil and to provide wisdom and instruction in order to close them quickly.

Find a home-cleansing prayer in Appendix C.

Generational Curses

Have you ever wondered why all the women in your family suffer from depression? Or perhaps in your family, as in mine, everyone has divorced at least once? Or are you puzzled that your family is continually living from paycheck to paycheck? Some of these ongoing struggles in our lives are the result of our own creation, yet a good number are the result of generational sin and curses.

I recall a season in my life when I engaged in earnest prayer work to become free of generational curses. I'd reviewed my family history, and to my astonishment, in every generation, as far back as I could uncover, a family member had suffered a premature death. And dreadfully, premature death traveled down both my father's and mother's family histories. In every generation someone died of disease, accident, or tragedy. And astonishingly, most were the firstborn male of the generation.

Say what?!

It's true. I concluded after much grieving prayer that the premature deaths in my family line were a direct result of Freemasonry curses.

I spent a good amount of time confessing, renouncing, and asking for forgiveness for participation by my ancestors in Masonry. After working through this part of my family history, I then inquired of the Lord to reveal any additional generational curses. Ugh! So much was revealed such as addictions, anger, alcoholism, adultery. Sheesh.

But I did the prayer work, and now I rest assured that this curse will not be passed down to my daughter, son, or grandchildren.

Generational iniquity and transgression are real. If you doubt this, just consider that humanity lives under a generational curse because of the sin of Adam and Eve. The Bible is very clear about this spiritual law as it was established.

So Moses chiseled out two stone tablets like the first ones and went up Mount Sinai early in the morning, as the Lord had commanded him; and he carried the two stone tablets in his hands. Then the Lord came down in the cloud and stood there with him and proclaimed his name, the Lord. And he passed in front of Moses, proclaiming, "The Lord, the Lord, the compassionate and gracious God, slow to anger, abounding in love and faithfulness, maintaining love to thousands, and forgiving wickedness, rebellion and sin. Yet he does not leave the guilty unpunished; he punishes the children and their children for the sin of the parents to the third and fourth generation. —Exodus 34:4–7 (emphasis mine)*

The law of unpunished sin is established in this passage. So what is the solution to law breaking?

The blood of Jesus. Our confession of sin and receiving the forgiveness of offenses against God is the process to release the grace of the Father and remove the evil contracts that exist in our families.

Generational sin is a common area that allows demonic oppression to continue from one generation to the next. Generational iniquity is perpetuated each time someone in the next generation sins in the same manner, which maintains the consequences on down the family line. That is until one brave believer in Christ takes a stand in the spirit realm and says, "No more!" They are determined to set themselves and their family free. They take on the prayer work to identify generational iniquity and pray through all of it, thereby receiving forgiveness for themselves and the generations that follow that is freely given through the cross.

Hallelujah!

Sex and Soul Ties

Sin against the body.

From God's perspective sin is sin. However, it's interesting that there are numerous scriptures that explicitly warn us against sexual sin. This particular sin not only affects the soul and spirit but is especially risky and dangerous to the body.

> *Run from sexual sin! No other sin so clearly affects the body as this one does. For sexual immorality is a sin against your own body. Don't you realize that your body is the temple of the Holy Spirit, who lives in you and was given to you by God? You do not belong to yourself, for God bought you with a high price. So you must honor God with your body.* — *1 Corinthians 6:18–20 (NLT)*

Sexual sin is not only rebellion against the Lord, but sexual sin releases rebellion, curses, and affliction into the physical body and specific body parts, finally becoming a generational curse.

The Bible is clear about sexual sin. Anything outside of married sex between a man and a woman is an invitation to the vast number of sexual demons that are always tempting and lurking. These demonic beasts, such as Lust, Perversion, Incubus, Succubus, and Lilith, move from one partner to another through illicit sex, including but not limited to intercourse. They also find entrance through pornography, explicit books, and novels.

Once this door opens, these evil beings delight in nighttime visits to create fear, molest, and immobilize an individual while they sleep. They are typically at the root of erotic sex dreams. I've gained this knowledge through my deliverance ministry.

I grieve over our hypersexed culture and the proliferation of pornography. Porn is now reaching our youngest children. It affects every aspect of our lives. Sex and pornography thrive on the internet, social media, all forms of advertising, children's libraries, and television.

Christians are also consuming pornography at growing rates, both men and women.

[Jesus] said, "For this reason a man shall leave his father and mother and be joined to his wife, and the two shall become one flesh." — Matthew 19:5 (NKJV)

Because sex joins a person to another, the two becoming one, a possible outcome of sex is the establishment of an emotional or soul bonding between the individuals. This bond may be mutual or only one-sided. These are spiritual soul ties.

Godly soul ties also exist between individuals in marriage. God blesses their bond of love and marital union. This spiritual bonding aids the commitment between the two. It protects their love, promotes and grows honor, respect, sacrifice, compassion, etc., between mates.

Typically, ungodly bonding is usually one-sided and holds a person captive to obsessive thoughts, which over time develop into unwelcome actions. Stalking, for example, is an ungodly soul tie in action.

I sometimes uncover these bonds during prayer sessions with a few diagnostic questions. I ask an individual if they compulsively think or dream about an ex-lover, ex-spouse, or even a friend. After a few more questions, we then pray and quickly terminate these evil spiritual bonds. Breaking soul ties is simply the renouncing and repentance of any sin with this partner, then asking Jesus to apply his blood to these sins and break all evil bonding.

Soul ties are also established outside sex. These form through mutual sin, drug use, criminal activity, controlling others, etc. But the ungodly and harmful bonds often are related to a sexual union.

Our culture is saturated with sexual temptation and the normalization of sexual sin. God really means it when he tells us to *run from sexual sin!* It's dangerous and will destroy you and your family.

For me, this is a mountain I'm willing to die on. I have strong boundaries in this area of my marriage. I'll acquiesce in other areas of disagreement with my husband, but sexual sin, pornography, or adultery is crossing a line that I will not abide.

It's difficult to tackle this subject because the world doesn't describe sexual sin in the way God does. And this is to the great delight of the demonic realm, who capitalize on this sin of the body. However, it's interesting to me that even among unsaved family members and marriage counselors, the majority conclude that infidelity and pornography are detrimental to a healthy marriage.

If your spouse is participating in sexual sin, it's time for another sit-down. First, talk to God about your marriage, your spouse, and your life. Seek help if you need it. Talk to a Christian counselor about confronting this kind of sin that is affecting your marriage.

False Religions

This is obvious to most believers that any religion outside of true Christianity is a quick road to deception and an open door to the Master Spirit that rules over that sect of a false religion. This is the most direct path to idol worship. Participating in false religious practices separates us from the presence of God.

> *The images of their gods you are to burn in the fire. Do not covet the silver and gold on them, and do not take it for yourselves,* or you will be ensnared by it, *for it is detestable to the Lord your God.* Do not bring a detestable thing into your house *or you, like it, will be set apart for destruction. Regard it as vile and utterly detest it, for it is set apart for destruction. —Deuteronomy 7:25–26 (emphasis mine)*

The deceptions are subtle in our world today. Remain alert when you hear statements such as "There is more than one path to God" or "Enlightenment is found in many places. Find your truth. You are your own god."

Many years ago, my mother was preparing to move from one state to another. She placed her home up for sale and expected that it would sell quickly. However, months passed. She received an offer at one point, but the buyer was illegitimate. This entire experience shook my mom. After months of no offers for her home and with her need to move rapidly approaching, she panicked.

She went to the store and purchased some kind of four-inch-tall saint and buried it in her front yard. Her neighbor had told her it would bring a buyer quickly.

When she told me what she did a few weeks later, I nearly threw up. Okay, I didn't, but my mom has been a believer in Jesus for more than fifty years. I was shocked that she would place hope in an inanimate object and then bury it in her yard, no less.

I quickly went to the front yard and pulled that thing up and tossed it in the garbage. It now resides in some dump heap in the Southwest. I knew my mom was desperate. And her friend, whom she loves and trusts, assured her this trinket would work. But after talking with me and reconsidering, she quickly realized this was looking to a false god and superstition instead of praying and believing Jesus had her in the palm of his hand.

Interestingly, her home sold a few weeks later and without the help of a superstitious yard idol. Probably because we prayed and repented, then asked the Lord to bring a qualified buyer.

It's possible that longtime believers might find themselves swept into deceit. Determine to subjugate panic, pressure, fear, and insecurity to the truth and dominion of our Lord.

Any religious practice or theology derived from a "sacred book" outside the Bible is a false religion. This is also true of any other deity or person other than the triune God.

If you have practiced a false religion or been in alignment with a religious spirit(s), find a repentance prayer in the next chapter and Appendix C.

Find a list of religious spirits and false religions in Appendix E.

Secrets and Secret Societies

"Lynn, I've never told anyone about this." When a person says this to me during a prayer session, I smile knowingly. I know what is about to happen. They are about to step into freedom.

Do you know why?

What hides in the darkness of personal secrets is fodder for evil. The demonic condemns and controls people through secret shame. A secret affair. Lying to a boss. The secret crime. An abortion. Or perhaps the molestation that happened when they were young. These are the untold, unrevealed, and concealed sins and trauma memories from our past. When they remain in darkness, evil manipulates secrets fostering shame, guilt, and unworthiness, which eventually leads to separation from the love of God. However, when confessed and brought out into the light, secret shame and sin lose their power! Hallelujah!

Speaking the hidden, in confession to another, frees a person to voice their shame and receive forgiveness and release from condemnation through Jesus. Often these confessions also release a person from physical afflictions, addictions, and fears. They are immediately released. It's really that simple.

And it's not.

Finding a trustworthy person who will not judge or condemn through this process is vital. This is the truth and power behind this Bible passage:

Therefore confess your sins to each other and pray for each other so that you may be healed. The prayer of a righteous person is powerful and effective. —James 5:16

Don't keep secrets. Don't deal in secrecy. Don't partner with deception.

Satan trades in secrets. When something is considered secret or there is some perceived "secret knowledge" only afforded a select few individuals, your gut check should be firing. Secrets are merely a distorted form of lying. The devil's same old, tired playbook. Sheesh!

Another form of secrecy that opens to demonic oppression are secret societies. These organizations present themselves as benevolent and beneficial to members and society. In actuality they are gateways that lead to deception and lies as a participant moves deeper into the organization.

For example, in Freemasonry an initiate often unknowingly speaks vows and pledges that have dire spiritual consequences. These vows authorize and empower demonic activity in the initiate's life as well as their family, affecting multiple generations.

These organizations promise "secret knowledge" and "advantages" over others. God loves all people. He doesn't give "advantages" to some people over others (Acts 10:34).

Personally, my family has suffered great loss due to involvement in Freemasonry. Any involvement by you or a family member in these clubs, societies, even some sororities and fraternities, is a potential open door. I could write a book about the sins of the fathers regarding secret societies; however, there isn't space or time for that in this volume. Research this topic yourself and discover what the Bible teaches about secrets and how the Word of God might apply to secret societies.

If you believe you or a family member is or was involved in a secret society, stop now. Get yourself or them out. Throw everything out associated with these organizations and repent. Locate a prayer ministry who can help you walk through freedom prayers from these types of curses and oppression.

Pray out loud:

Father, in the name of Jesus, I come before your throne of Grace to receive grace and mercy this hour. Father, I confess, repent, and renounce on behalf of myself and my ancestors for their involvement in any secret societies [name them here if you know the name of the society. Be as detailed as possible]. *Forgive my family members for speaking oaths to anyone or anything other than you, the true Lord of all, Yahweh. I confess this is idol worship, and I grieve over this rebellion in our family. Please forgive us and wash these iniquities from our family name and remove all blood guilt. Remove and cancel all evil that was empowered through these vows, pledges, and rituals.*

Jesus, your blood is redemption and I receive the cleansing of all sin, transgression, and iniquity on behalf of myself and my family bloodline. Today I declare we are set free. I break the power and all contracts with evil right now and declare freedom over us. Now, Lord Jesus, please bless our family for a thousand generations with righteousness, good-ness, peace, wholeness, and bless us to follow hard after you. In your mighty name, Jesus, amen!

Occult

Occult practices of any kind are wide open doors. Witchcraft spells, ritu-als, and participation in devil worship invites demonic infestation. It's a certainty. Occult practices are empowered by demons.

Unfortunately, the avenues into the occult are often unassuming. Something as simple as "saging" your home or hanging a dream catcher, playing with a Ouija board, even certain video games, will open a pathway to darkness. Many of these practices are entry into witchcraft.

If you have participated in anything of the occult, repent and ask Jesus for your freedom. Throw out everything you used to practice witchcraft or the occult. Schedule a deliverance prayer session.

Avoid like a plague the following: tarot readings, mediums, seances, palm readers, and such. These activities are becoming commonplace at work or company picnics, office gatherings, and other large events.

Talismans

The English language may have borrowed the word *talisman* from French, Spanish, or Italian; all three include similar-looking words to mean a lucky charm that derive from an Arabic word for a charm, *țilsam*. Țilsam traces to the ancient Greek word *telein*, which means "to initiate into the mysteries." —Merrium-Webster.

Talismans are objects that are believed to confer magic, offer good or bad luck, or hold supernatural power. These objects in themselves may not hold any kind of supernatural power. But again, it's what we believe in our heart that empowers a spirit through an object.

For example, if I were to purchase a crystal, it's merely a pretty rock. I don't have any belief in supernatural power, luck, or protection outside the kingdom of God. However, there are millions of people who purchase crystals because they believe they bring luck, fortune, good energy, and especially protection to themselves or to the dwelling where they are placed.

Another example of the effect of a talisman occurs more frequently than you might believe. Let's consider the fictional couple, the Larsons. This Christian couple saved for years to finally take a dream vacation to the Orient. They visit a number of Buddhist, Hindu, and other East Asian temples as part of their itinerary. These are well-visited tourist sites, each uniquely beautiful and highlighted as a "must-see" in the travel brochure. They stop at a gift shop and find a stylish and expensive replica of a pretty Hindu shrine and pack it home where it now sits atop the fireplace mantle.

What they don't realize is that this trinket was "blessed," or perhaps the correct word is "cursed," by the temple priest in the name of the god he serves. Upon arriving home, the Larsons begin experiencing a number of unexpected and uncanny disasters. Unexplained breakage of a few major appliances. Mold is discovered in the basement. They seem always to be tired and have had nightmares since they returned.

They finally conclude that something is not right in their house and call their pastor. Fortunately, the pastor is well aware that demonic attachment is real. He quickly pinpoints the shrine on the fireplace as the problem. The Larsons dispatch it to the garbage where it belongs. They repent, then cleanse their house with oil, followed by blessing, and receive their peaceful home back.

It's easy to fall into this kind of deception. It's the motive and belief behind our actions. We might have thoughts such as "It just might bring me luck," "It can't hurt to hang a dream catcher over my child's bed at night to protect him from nightmares," or "What can it hurt to check my daily horoscope?"

The motive of the heart reflects our beliefs. These objects range from the mostly harmless to occult figures and insignia that are portals of access.

Cadet, we are building our house on a strong platform and creating an impenetrable defense against marauders who want to destroy our faith, home, and family. Keeping these trinkets, books, candles, and ornaments that represent ungodliness and a supernatural power other than Yahweh weakens us, and we become casualties on the battleground.

Get rid of them. And now.

The topics I've shared with you in this chapter are the most common areas where humanity opens a door to demonic activity. But it's not everything. Stay alert. Your intimate relationship with Jesus will protect you. The Holy Spirit will gut-check you when you come up against something that is hosting evil.

Now that we have a glimpse of the evil realm's intents and purposes as well as strategies, we have greater insight into our interactions and situations within our marriage, in our family relationships, and in our homes. We now possess knowledge and wisdom regarding the evil realm's attack patterns. Knowledge coupled with our authority offers us great power to defeat darkness.

Remember, we are blood-bought, powerful children of the King. We have been prepared for the fight. We walk in great authority and power of the Holy Spirit. We are living right now in this season of the epic battle of all eternity and are expected to kick butt and take names. Our family generations are at stake. We have the truth. And the truth frees us, our family, and the generations that follow.

It's a great time to be alive and in the kingdom of God!

Ephesians 6

Take up the shield of faith, with which you can extinguish all the flaming arrows of the evil one.

Chapter Nine
IDOL WORSHIP

You shall have no other gods before me.—Exodus 20:3

C adet, we are more than halfway through the enforcement academy. It's intense. We have conquered many fears and left doubt behind. We are covert missionaries who are discerning the times, the atmospheres, and the evil that lurks. We've gained mighty tools and truths to the pulling down of strongholds and lies. We walk as ambassadors of God with our weapons readied and our victory certain.

In the next area of training, we advance to become specialists. Let's tackle one of the most subtle strongholds of deception of the satanic kingdom, idol worship.

In Western cultures, idol worship is viewed as superstitious and archaic. Bowing before a physical idol such as a carved image or bowing to the sun, moon or stars, etc. isn't commonplace in our day-to-day life. And as believers, our knee never bows to any supernatural power other than Yahweh.

Yet idol worship is deceptively thriving in our Western cultures and among believers. Many Christians are caught up in idol worship unknowingly. Without remedy, our Ephesians 6 armor is vulnerable.

And this is why.

Exodus 20.

God's laws were established to benefit humanity and to prosper people who are committed to his kingdom.

And God spoke all these words, saying:

"I am the Lord your God, who brought you out of the land of Egypt, out of the house of bondage.

"You shall have no other gods before Me.

"You shall not make for yourself a carved image—any likeness of anything that is in heaven above, or that is in the earth beneath, or that is in the water under the earth; you shall not bow down to them nor serve them. For I, the Lord your God, am a jealous God, visiting the iniquity of the fathers upon the children to the third and fourth generations of those who hate Me, but showing mercy to thousands, to those who love Me and keep My commandments." —Exodus 20:1–6 (NKJV, emphasis mine)

This is the first of the Ten Commandments. It is a primary spiritual law. Spiritual laws exist in tandem with the natural laws, such as the laws of physics. We are affected by both.

In the natural realm, we experience the law of gravity 24/7. Humanity has learned to manipulate gravity, but we continually feel the effects of its force.

God established physical laws for the universe at creation. He also established spiritual laws. Both are irrefutable regardless of our awareness or acknowledgment of their existence. They are unchangeable.

Humanity experiences the benefits and penalties of complying with or breaking these eternal statutes, as does every being in the spiritual realm (Psalm 111:7–8).

But you may be thinking, *Lynn, as new covenant believers, we don't live under the law.*

You are correct. As believers we have been *forgiven the penalty of the law* because of Jesus. But forgiveness doesn't negate the fact that the laws and penalties remain in full effect. Jesus affirms this truth when he said:

Spiritual Enforcer

Do not think that I came to destroy the Law or the Prophets. I did not come to destroy but to fulfill. For assuredly, I say to you, till heaven and earth pass away, one jot or one tittle will by no means pass from the law till all is fulfilled. Whoever therefore breaks one of the least of these commandments, and teaches men so, shall be called least in the kingdom of heaven; but whoever does and teaches them, he shall be called great in the kingdom of heaven. —Matthew 5:17–19 (NKJV)

When God's spiritual laws are broken, our path back to God is the new covenant. This covenant overrides the old covenant, the law. Our covenant was sealed, adopted, and approved through the blood atonement of Jesus!

We access Christ's atonement through faith, through confession and belief in the finished work of the cross. We find forgiveness for sin, the breaking of God's law, in Jesus, the Christ. Hallelujah! Blessed be God!

We are forgiven when we confess, repent, and ask for forgiveness. The penalty of the law no longer retains a legal right or hold on us. It's truly astonishing!

So what is the penalty for breaking the first spiritual law, "have no other gods before me"?

If there is found among you, within any of your gates which the Lord your God gives you, a man or a woman who has been wicked in the sight of the Lord your God, in transgressing His covenant, who has gone and served other gods and worshiped them, *either the sun or moon or any of the host of heaven, which I have not commanded, and it is told you, and you hear of it, then you shall inquire diligently. And if it is indeed true and certain that such an abomination has been committed in Israel, then you shall bring out to your gates that man or woman who has committed that wicked thing, and shall* stone to death *that man or woman with stones. —Deuteronomy 17:2–5 (NKJV, emphasis mine)*

The penalty for rebellion (i.e., idol worship) is death.

Now, this is where understanding the legalities of the spiritual kingdom becomes interesting. God's laws, statues, and penalties continu-

93

ally apply to all of humanity. Serving another god, such as the god of Mammon, Lucifer, false religions etc., releases the death penalty. Literally, a door in the spiritual realm of our soul opens for the spirit of death to infiltrate, beginning with our thoughts. Over time it whispers, *No one loves you. No one cares if you are here. You would be better off in heaven. Life is too hard.*

As an individual begins to believe the lies and align with the false narrative, they experience greater exposure to affliction, illness, poverty and more. The enemy has gained legal access to develop self-loathing, hatred of others, blaming God, eventually leading to premature death or disease. Whoa!

My little children, these things I write to you, so that you may not sin. And if anyone sins, we have an Advocate with the Father, Jesus Christ the righteous. —*1 John 2:1 (NKJV)*

Jesus is our legal advocate, our defender. Our confession, repentance, and receiving of forgiveness is our remedy, breaking the power of the law. The sacrifice of Christ on the cross is the payment for our transgression, our penalty. The curses released because of idol worship, such as Freemasonry, the occult, false religions, etc. are nullified. Jesus paid the price. Therefore, when we have no other gods before Yahweh, we live in peace, divine health, prosperity, and love. We live out of the promises of God.

Wow . . . just wow!

Our responsibility is to apprehend forgiveness through earnest confession, repentance, and renouncement.

With this history lesson in mind, it becomes incredibly important that we know what God views as a false god. I think the best way to determine if we have a god that is above our Father in heaven is to take a survey of our heart.

Above all else, guard your heart, for everything you do flows from it. — *Proverbs 4:23*

It's out of our heart that we perceive life.

If we believe that a crystal placed in our home brings good energy, we have ascribed to a supernatural power, a "belief" to another god. If we think Reiki will heal our body, we have chosen a demonic power over our healer, Jesus. If we have more faith in our own strength, wisdom, charisma, and intellect than in the Lord, we have crossed a line.

I have walked with God consistently now for decades. The longer I follow hard after him, the more extreme I become about having no other gods before him. I've repented over watching certain movies, speaking words of sickness over myself, and ungodly friendships. I've repented for participation in activities I once thought silly and harmless: tossing salt over my shoulder, relying on lucky numbers, reading my horoscope, keeping a rabbit's foot for luck. Ack! Egads! Whoever thought a dead rabbit's foot was lucky? I don't know, but ick!

Now, remember, I am only a messenger. I am not condemning. What you choose in your life is between you and the Father, Jesus, and Holy Spirit. But if you are tired of losing battles with the devil, if you are weary and don't understand why God isn't responding to your prayers, perhaps it's time to reevaluate *what HE THINKS* about idol worship.

Remember, the higher we move into purity of heart, belief, and practice, the more we draw upon the power and authority of Christ.

I want more power and authority. I want to set people free. I greatly desire to heal the sick, cleanse the lepers, cast out demons, and raise the dead. With all of my heart, I want God's kingdom on earth and to glorify my Father in heaven.

This is my simple motivation.

And now you have the truth. The devil continues to deceive and destroy the church through subtle offerings to turn from faith in God to an idol.

For rebellion is as the sin of witchcraft, and stubbornness is as iniquity and idolatry. Because you have rejected the word of the Lord, He also has rejected you from being king. —1 Samuel 15:23 (NKJV)

Rebellion through idol worship is serious business. Read the list of practices in Appendix D that can become a god in a person's heart. Remember, it's about the heart and your belief about supernatural power or favor. Then pray and ask the Lord to reveal if anything from the list has been in your history or that of your family. Then own it. Acknowledge that you participated. Confess, repent, and renounce it all.

Renouncing is turning completely from the practice and belief.

Pray aloud:

Father, in the name of Jesus, I confess that I have knowingly or unknowingly offered my heart, my belief, or my hope to any god other than you. I grieve that I have rebelled against your wise statutes, and I have hurt your heart. I repent for participating in any way physically, with my body. I repent for offering my soul or spirit to any foreign god. I ask for your forgiveness for _____ [insert specifics and pray as the Holy Spirit leads].

I also confess and ask for forgiveness on behalf of my ancestors for any way they participated in idol worship. Please forgive all of us. Please cleanse our family name and forgive our blood guilt. I now apply the blood of Jesus to these sins, and I receive the forgiveness that he purchased on my behalf. I also receive his healing and freedom. Now reunite me into your heart, Father.

Holy Spirit, lead me to depend on the power and love of the Father wholly and faithfully as my only source for help, protection, provision, love, and acceptance.

I pledge my loyalty, my love, my service here on earth and eternally to you, Father. In the mighty, saving name of Jesus, amen!

Find a list of religious spirits and false religious practices in the appendices.

Spiritual Enforcer

Ephesians 6

Take up the shield of faith, with which you can extinguish all the flaming arrows of the evil one.

Part Three
Taking Back the House

*Therefore take up the whole armor of God, that you may be able to
withstand in the evil day, and having done all, to stand
Stand therefore, having girded your waist with truth, having put on the
breastplate of righteousness, and having shod your feet with the
preparation of the gospel of peace; above all, taking the shield of faith
with which you will be able to quench all the fiery darts of the wicked*

one. And take the helmet of salvation, and the sword of the Spirit, which is the word of God; praying always with all prayer and supplication in the Spirit, being watchful to this end with all perseverance and supplication for all the saints. —Ephesians 6:13–18 (NKJV)

Chapter Ten
WAR AND ENFORCER POWER TOOLS

*For the weapons of our warfare are not carnal but mighty in God
for pulling down strongholds, casting down arguments and every
high thing that exalts itself against the knowledge of God,
bringing every thought into captivity to the obedience of Christ,
and being ready to punish all disobedience when your obedience
is fulfilled. —2 Corinthians 10:4–6 (NKJV)*

Three dots and a dash . . . —
Cue the war cry. VICTORY!

God provides powerful tools, armor, and an offensive weapon that is stronger "than any double-edged sword [and] penetrates even to dividing soul and spirit, joints and marrow; it judges the thoughts and attitudes of the heart" (Hebrews 4:12). In this section of our training, we are gaining momentum as we pick up additional armor and weapons that destroy the works of darkness.

The remainder of our tactical uniform is found in Ephesians 6. As spiritual enforcers we expect pushback, assaults, and plots of evil. However, it's possible to sustain a direct shot to the chest and remain victorious as we are ensconced in these valuable protections.

Breastplate of Righteousness

Lynn Donovan

Stand therefore, having girded your waist with truth, having put on the breastplate of righteousness. —Ephesians 6:14 (NKJV)

At the core of our faith is our heart. For out of our heart the mouth speaks (Luke 6:45). Our heart affects our decisions, attitudes, emotional and physical health, and voice. It is where we receive love and the well from which we impart love to others. The breastplate of righteousness is love. It is the covering of our heart.

A lifestyle of love is the highest and best life. Love covers a multitude of sins, infractions, disappointments, and change. Loving others, even the most difficult people, becomes possible and easier when we understand we are wholly and completely loved by a good Father. Out of this awareness our desire to live rightly (righteousness) is born and developed. Adorning this breastplate of heaven becomes a powerful positioning in the kingdom realm. Our authority in Christ branches out from us singularly to everyone and everything that falls under our love, stewardship, and jurisdiction.

This shield protects our heart, out of which flow our thoughts, desires, and hopes.

Righteousness is developed through a practice of reading the Scriptures and conforming ourselves to the image of Christ. It is the practice of quick obedience. It is the deep desire to love and pursue Jesus above all else. We develop our breastplate through dying to self, releasing our immature and unrealized worldly expectations of ourselves, our spouse, and others. We gain powerful protection when we decide we are "all in" and will no longer compromise.

This isn't easy to walk out, trainee. We will bump up against people who oppose our changing stance and growing faith. But becoming a true enforcement officer is a single-minded, lifetime commitment. And it *is* doable, even within an unequally yoked marriage.

What I know to be true is when we remain unrelenting in our consistent practice of faith, others will slowly, perhaps begrudgingly, begin to abide in our new strength. They will eventually respect our faith, and they will eventually be affected by who we are and all that we carry inside.

They can't help but be changed because we are changed. I'm speaking from decades of experience. This is the hope we cling to when experiencing disappointment or setbacks.

Shoes of Peace

Shod your feet with the preparation of the gospel of peace. — Ephesians 6:15 (NKJV)

Did you know the devil can simulate emotions? For example, he can mirror love, happiness, joy, and power. But the one thing the devil cannot create is peace.

Humanity longs for peace. As we mature in faith, our yearning for greater peace becomes compelling. We were never made for chaos, discord, and fighting. Our soul instinctively desires to live in the atmosphere of heavenly peace.

But how do we find peace?

Once again, this isn't really the correct question.

It's up to us to create and steward peace. But how? This is the correct question. And I'm glad you asked. *grin*

The answer is to use our powerful voice and release blessings and peace. I mentioned this practice in chapter 5.

Nearly every prayer I utter in my life today is a blessing prayer. Unless I am going to battle for a person or circumstance, I'm usually speaking blessing prayers. I bless in the morning. I bless at noonday. I bless in the evening. I bless so much that Mike hears me praying aloud while I'm asleep, mumbling blessings into the dark. Weird but cool! Poor Mike! I guess that's better than snoring. *grin*

We receive authority to bless through Scripture.

Bless those who persecute you; bless and do not curse. Rejoice with those who rejoice; mourn with those who mourn. Live in harmony with one another. Do not be proud, but be willing to associate with people of low position. Do not be conceited. Do not repay anyone evil for evil. Be careful to do what is right in the eyes of everyone. If it is possible, as far as it depends on you, live at peace with everyone. —Romans 12:14–18 (emphasis mine)

These scriptures empower us to bless like Jesus. He modeled blessing in Matthew 5. Remember, our authority to bless comes from Jesus. We always bless in his name.

We literally have the power and authority to change—no, let me restate—to set the emotional, physical, and spiritual atmosphere of our home, our workplace, anywhere we have jurisdiction. Just like a police officer who arrives on scene and restores peace and safety, this is also our responsibility and calling. It is absolutely possible. This is our Father's expectation for his mature sons and daughters.

I covered blessing prayers in my last book, *Marching Around Jericho*. But since that publication, I've come to understand that blessing prayers are often part of a two-part demonstration of the Holy Spirit's power and Christ's authority.

When we are facing a circumstance that challenges our peace, home, or stance, our responsibility is to take authority over the situation. But the second part of taking authority or binding an evil intruder is to release blessing.

This process is outlined in Scripture.

"When an impure spirit comes out of a person, it goes through arid places seeking rest and does not find it. Then it says, 'I will return to the house I left.' When it arrives, it finds the house unoccupied, swept clean and put in order. Then it goes and takes with it seven other spirits more wicked than itself, and they go in and live there. And the final condition of that person is worse than the first. That is how it will be with this wicked generation." —Matthew 12:43–45

When we take authority over something, let's say chaos, we remove it with our commanding prayers. We forbid chaos from returning and then speak or pray a blessing of peace into our mind and over our home.

Our blessing fills the abandoned space with the attributes of our Father. Therefore, if unwanted violators attempt a return, the door is closed.

This is a two-pronged prayer approach. I've found this prayer method highly effective.

The first key to successful engagement is recognition. Ask the Lord for awareness. We must train ourselves to rapidly discern when something is out of alignment with God's values. Then ask the Lord to reveal what is at hand. Gaining this prayer and discernment ability requires practice.

When we are embroiled in a heated conversation or chaos is swirling about, or when a troubling and fast-paced circumstance unfolds, our ability to identify what lurks behind the circumstance becomes challenging. Therefore, practice discernment proactively.

Here's some practical practice: During morning prayer ask the Lord to equip and develop your sensitivity to discern the truth of spiritual and natural surroundings and people. Also, ask the Holy Spirit to provide you with tactics for enforcement with kingdom results. Then throughout the day, practice discerning the spiritual reality regarding people you encounter and the atmospheres where you live and work.

Secondly, when discerning a spirit, speak aloud, commanding it to depart. Finally, follow up with a release, a blessing, of the opposite spirit. Always in the name of Jesus.

Here are several common difficulties as well as examples of how to pray specifically:

The spirit of delay. Regularly the demonic realm will create delays in life that perpetuate fear, contributing to confusion and hopelessness. For example, a delay in the delivery of a promise from an employer or friend, the arrival of a passport or check in the mail, etc. So many delays impact our lives. However, a delay in the natural is often the result of a demonic blockage in the unseen realm.

Recently, a friend of mine was scheduled to fly to America for a stay at my home in California. She was toting along her young daughter. Prior to her trip, she applied for her youngster's passport, but it didn't arrive, didn't arrive, didn't arrive, until finally it became concerningly late. She emailed me a message about her frustration over the delay. The next morning, I went straight into enforcer mode.

Lord Jesus, by your name, I take authority over this spirit of delay that has bogged down this passport for_____ [I said her name]. Lord, this is wrong. This visit is in your will, and this mom and daughter will be blessed. So today I command this spirit of delay that is holding this passport at the Canadian passport authority to RELEASE it. I stand in faith for this family with love in my heart. I declare this delay is broken now in the spiritual realm, and this passport will be mailed right now.

Also, Jesus, I assign and dispatch angels immediately to this office where this passport is approved. Work with and bless the people who approve this passport and urge them to finish their work. I bless them with peace and a manageable workload, that they find favor over [my friend's name]. Now I bless this passport to arrive in time for travel. And bless everyone who has their hands or authority over it. In Your powerful name, Jesus, amen!

PS. It arrived and our visit was wonderful.

The spirit of pride. This becomes obvious as we face pride around nearly every corner of society and within our family relationships.

Jesus, I humble myself before you. I refuse to partner with the deceptions of pride and arrogance. I wholly lean on the truth of your authoritative Word. Therefore, I bind this boasting spirit and the spirit of conflict who are speaking arrogantly against the truth. I take authority over pride, arrogance, narcissism, and envy and the root of it all, fear. I cast each of these spirits down, along with every high thing that exalts itself against the knowledge of God. I now bring every thought into captivity to the obedience of Christ and being ready to punish all disobedience when your obedience is fulfilled. Pride cannot stand against your name and authority.

I silence and rebuke pride, in Jesus's name.

Now, Lord Jesus, I release the angelic and the spirit of peace along with humility and honor into [name place, circumstance, or person] right now. Holy Spirit, manifest your peace and your presence in me and around me. Peace shall reign because that is the mandate of heaven. Of the greatness of your government and peace there will be no end.

In the powerful, ruling name of Jesus, the King of glory, amen!

Let's partner with those who are for us and who are available to fight on our side for the kingdom of righteousness and peace.

Now I bless you today to receive this new tool and use it often. Hallelujah! AMEN!

The spirit of manipulation. This ugly spirit is rooted in witchcraft. The foundation of witchcraft is the control of another, to subvert free will and manipulate a person or people to conform to the controller's desires. Even typing this sentence, it reeks of satanic agendas.

We witness control in action as it exerts itself over the masses from the highest levels of global governments all the way down to the control or manipulation within our jobs, marriages and even in our churches. As believers we are not immune to this manipulative motivation.

Ugh!

God hates this spirit because it propagates through sly deceptions, questions of doubt, deceit, and half-truths. It's insidious and lurks even within our own minds. It's empowered through fear and unpredictability.

Let's consider a few diagnostic questions. Do you witness agendas that are ungodly occurring in your child's school? What about in your workplace? Do you hear manipulation coming from the television or perhaps from your husband's mouth or your own?

Take authority over this beast and command it to come under the dominion of Jesus Christ. Demand that it submit its rebellious posture and propagation to the rulership of the iron rod of Jesus (Revelation 2:27). Command the spirit to be silent. Defeated. Destroyed. Dismantled. And every other thing the Holy Spirit reveals. Then release the blessings of mutual honor, respect, love, service, and sacrifice into the situation.

In the name of Jesus, I bless this school, office, home, government with the mind of Christ. I bless this place/organization to be inundated with love and kindness, honor, and respect. I bless this person(s) to be a person of compassion and be filled with a heart of mercy, service, and sacrifice. I bless this government/workplace, etc. to value freedom and peace. In the mighty name of Jesus, amen!

I bet you didn't know this extraordinary position of power and authority belongs to those who wear the shoes of the gospel of peace.

My friend, the next time you lace up your shoes, think upon these things. Then smile. The world belongs to those who seek and serve the gospel of peace.

Blessed are the meek, for they shall inherit the earth. —Matthew 5:5 (NKJV)

Take time to practice recognizing what you are truly facing. Depose evil and disband all legal rights, then bless the people and situation involved.

The Shield of Faith

Above all, [take] the shield of faith with which you will be able to quench all the fiery darts of the wicked one. —Ephesians 6:16 (NKJV)

Our tactical uniform, along with our badge and weapon, form our faith shield. We camped on this subject in detail in chapter 1.

Every day you will face choices. Choices, choices, choices. We make hundreds a day. But the most important choice you make every day is choosing faith over fear. And belief over doubt. *This is the shield of faith!* And faith protects us, our family, and home from the fiery darts of evil spirits, lies, deception, and unbelief.

The Helmet

And take the helmet of salvation. —Ephesians 6:17 (NKJV)

Spiritual Enforcer

The helmet of salvation is broader than most believe. Large portions of the church consider salvation a moment in time when a person makes a profession of faith in Jesus. They receive forgiveness of their sin, and when they die, they go to heaven for eternity. And this is absolutely true. However, salvation is more than a one and done. It's truly a lifetime of saving. Hallelujah.

> *Therefore, my dear friends, as you have always obeyed—not only in my presence, but now much more in my absence—continue* to work out your salvation *with fear and trembling. —Philippians 2:12 (emphasis mine)*

Paul is urging the church of Philippi to continue to appropriate and receive their salvation. This is an encouraging truth for us today. We are continually saved.

Through my own maturing process, I still uncover broken mind-sets and lies that need healing and truth. I need saving again and again. My salvation is an ongoing, day-to-day love pursuit of this one man, Jesus.

Jesus is incredibly interested in our ongoing salvation. After all, the whipping post was an extreme purchase so that we may live in continual healing and freedom. And his death gave us life. Life abundantly now on earth and eternal life with our Father and his children.

Our salvation, our joining the academy and becoming kingdom enforcers, is the core of our triumph over this world and over evil. We must sign on the dotted line in the Lamb's Book of Life and live a sold-out life of loyalty from that point forward. This is the helmet that guards our minds and hearts from deception, weariness, persecution, and doubt.

I often affirm my loyalty to the Lord in my morning prayer time. It's a high privilege to pledge loyalty to the King of Kings. And I don't take my pledge, responsibilities, and privileges lightly. Living from this place of faith, with my helmet securely upon my head, I dispel lies and deceptions that would lead me from my path of purpose.

Hallelujah! Thank you for the cross!

The Sword

The sword of the Spirit, which is the word of God. —Ephesians 6:17 (NKJV)

Entire books are written about the sword of the Spirit. I hope to share enough for you to grasp the power and freedom that is available to us through the Word of God.

To fully utilize this weapon of offense, we must first comprehend that God is life. Our Father's essence is life and life-giving. If God appears on the scene, life is imminent. Everything about the ministry of Jesus (God-man) pointed us to the Father and to life. He healed the sick, blind, and lame, thereby releasing life and creative miracles that flow from the Father. He cast out demons, breaking chains of bondage and suffering that lead to physical and spiritual death, thereby releasing life.

God is life: "*In Him was life*, and the life was the light of men" (John 1:4 NKJV, emphasis mine)

Jesus is life: "Jesus said to him, 'I am the way, the truth, and *the life*. No one comes to the Father except through Me'" (John 14:6 NKJV, emphasis mine).

Holy Spirit is life: "For the law of the *Spirit of life* in Christ Jesus has made me free from the law of sin and death" (Romans 8:2 NKJV, emphasis mine).

If our mandate is to bring God's kingdom to earth, we partner with life, the "living" Word.

For the word of God is alive and active. Sharper than any double-edged sword, it penetrates even to dividing soul and spirit, joints and marrow; it judges the thoughts and attitudes of the heart. —Hebrews 4:12 (emphasis mine)

Why is it vitally important to partner with the living Word? Because everything around us is under the curse of the evil one and exists in some degree of dying or death.

Spiritual Enforcer

The thief comes only to steal and kill and destroy; I have come that they may have life, and have it to the full. —John 10:10

Central to spiritual warfare is this passage in John. The devil's ministry is to steal, kill, and destroy. Jesus came to release life. Through the power and authority of Christ, we release life through the living words of God, the Bible. We displace the works of darkness when we partner with truth and release the life of the Father into our jurisdiction.

When we speak Scripture into a situation through our commanding prayers partnered with our faith and belief, we are empowering the words of God into reality. The Bible is literally God's voice. His authoritative voice. And he's made his words available for us to speak into this world. And within the Scriptures, we discover everything we need for life and godliness (2 Peter 1:3).

The apostle Paul equated the Word with a sword. Kingdom enforcers, visualize our firearms raised as we partner with the Holy Spirit to dismantle and destroy evil. Believe the words of life are flying from the end of our weapons. Point our will (intentions and purpose) toward a matter, and release the Scriptures.

This weaponry is our most powerful opposition to every evil we confront.

Do you recall the prayer I shared in chapter 7? We prayed a passage straight out of Ephesians. This is an example of praying Scripture back to our Father. But the Word offers us much more. Take a look at this example.

Several years ago, I was lying in bed and couldn't sleep. My nose was plugged up for some reason, which didn't make any sense to me. So, out of frustration and because I was tired and needed sleep, I put my fingers on the bridge of my nose and said aloud with passionate force, "Sinuses, be loosed! In Jesus's name." And I flung my fingers away from my face as if loosening something from my nose.

I believed this passage in the book of Matthew.

And I will give you the keys of the kingdom of heaven, and whatever you
bind on earth will be bound in heaven, and whatever you loose on earth
will be loosed in heaven. —*Matthew 16:19 (NKJV, emphasis mine)*

What I loose on earth, I believe, is backed up by heaven. Immediately, my sinuses began to drain. My nose cleared up within minutes, and I drifted off to sleep with a smile on my face.

I practice this scripture often. It's incredibly powerful. I bind devils that are hindering my progress or my prayer work and interfering with my life. I loose life into situations. I've loosed life into a dead bird who crashed into my family room window and then blessed it in Jesus's name. The sweet thing popped up, shook its feathers, and flew off. Currently, I'm practicing my faith by blessing dead trees back to life. I like to practice the Word of God in partnership with the Holy Spirit. I pray and command the Word of God into so many aspects of my life.

Side note: I greatly encourage you to study and read from a printed form of the Bible. Studies and my personal experience have concluded that retention is greater when we read from paper or print as opposed to a digital form. Read from a good ole fashioned print Bible. Let life flow from the pages and receive the benefits.

Another fantastic aspect of praying the Word of God is this: our prayers open up a partnership with the angelic realm.

Bless the Lord, you His angels, who excel in strength, who do His word,
heeding the voice of His word. —Psalm 103:20 (NKJV, emphasis mine)

Are they not all ministering spirits sent forth to minister for those who
will inherit salvation? —Hebrews 1:14 (NKJV)

The *most* powerful position in prayer is releasing Scripture into the unseen realm. When we pray Scripture back to God or into a circumstance, we are literally echoing the voice of God. And when we do, angels become interested in our prayers. Scripture empowers the angelic to move on our behalf. Believe it!

Let's make this real right now. Consider an area of change you need in your life. Write it below:

_____

_____

_____

_____

_____

_____

Date:

Now, look up the scriptures that speak to truth regarding your situation. Write them out.

_____

_____

_____

_____

_____

Speak the scriptures with faith and with command into your situation.

Write them on a three-by-five card or in your phone, and keep them with you. Refuse to partner with doubt and fear, and continually pray these scriptures aloud into your circumstance, believing God's words facilitate change. Worship God for his intervention and love. Give thanks that he is moving on your behalf.

Worship and praise empower the prayers of his people.

Remember to kick the devil out first. Then release life abundantly.

Finally, and more importantly, remember to give the Lord thanks when he answers. Tell others about his faithfulness. Our testimony releases life, faith, and hope into our future in great measure as well into the lives of others.

Let me share a quick example of biblical prayers for unsaved family members.

Prayer need: Husband's and children's salvation.

Scriptures:

The Lord is not slow in keeping his promise, as some understand slowness. Instead he is patient with you, not wanting anyone to perish, but everyone to come to repentance. —2 Peter 3:9

The goodness of God leads you to repentance. —Romans 2:4 (NKJV)

Prayer:

Father, your Word says that you don't want my husband or children to perish but to live and come to repentance and faith in Jesus. I am believing this Word and declare it over my spouse and children [speak their names aloud]. I ask for and believe they shall have an encounter with your love and goodness. They shall experience your love and know you are kind and have planned a good life for them. I know you keep your promises; therefore, I stand in faith for their deliverance, freedom, and salvation. In the mighty name of Jesus, our Savior, amen.

Cadet, we've concluded our classroom training from the book of Ephesians. We reviewed a ton of information. Significant practice and belief are ahead as you take on these weapons and armor. But I promise you this: put these principles, the teaching, and truths into practice, and you will partner with Lord and participate in phenomena that astound and bless you and others.

Spiritual Enforcer

Ephesians 6

Take up the shield of faith, with which you can extinguish all the flaming arrows of the evil one.

Chapter Eleven
ENFORCER TOOLS

For the weapons of our warfare are not carnal but mighty in God
for pulling down strongholds, casting down arguments and every
high thing that exalts itself against the knowledge of God,
bringing every thought into captivity to the obedience of Christ,
and being ready to punish all disobedience when your obedience
is fulfilled. —2 Corinthians 10:4–6 (NKJV)

Power Tools of Kingdom Enforcers

B efore we move forward into the next area of study, let's summarize
the primary power tools of an enforcer. Please note: specific
teaching regarding the four-pronged approach to forgiveness is outlined
in *Marching Around Jericho*, so I did not include it in this book.

The tools are basic theological truths from the Word. They encapsu-
late the lifestyle of a believer who desires to live like Christ.

Number One: Love

I pray that you, being rooted and established in love, may have power, together with all the Lord's holy people, to grasp how wide and long and high and deep is the love of Christ, and to know this love that surpasses knowledge—that you may be filled to the measure of all the fullness of God. —Ephesians 3:17–19

Everything about our Father in heaven, Jesus our Savior, and the entire kingdom of God is centered in his perfect love.

There is no fear in love. But perfect love drives out fear, because fear has to do with punishment. The one who fears is not made perfect in love. — 1 John 4:18

The totality of our life experience ultimately leads us to this question: did we learn to love? Do we love God and love people? Because of my past, I always feel as though I'm living out of a love deficit. I ask God to love on me frequently. I ask to experience his love, feel his love, know his love. And in response, he pours out upon me with an unending flow. I'm a very needy child of God. So are you.

Recruit, you can't give out what you don't have. This is why we ask for greater revelation of God's love. It's out of the overflow that we are able to love others and to learn to love them well.

This is love in action:

Love must be sincere. Hate what is evil; cling to what is good. Be devoted to one another in love. Honor one another above yourselves. Never be lacking in zeal, but keep your spiritual fervor, serving the Lord. Be joyful in hope, patient in affliction, faithful in prayer. Share with the Lord's people who are in need. Practice hospitality.

Bless those who persecute you; bless and do not curse. Rejoice with those who rejoice; mourn with those who mourn. Live in harmony with one another. Do not be proud, but be willing to associate with people of low position. Do not be conceited.

Do not repay anyone evil for evil. Be careful to do what is right in the eyes of everyone. If it is possible, as far as it depends on you, live at peace with everyone. Do not take revenge, my dear friends, but leave room for God's wrath, for it is written: "It is mine to avenge; I will repay," says the Lord. On the contrary: "If your enemy is hungry, feed him; if he is thirsty, give him something to drink. In doing this, you will heap burning coals on his head."

Do not be overcome by evil, but overcome evil with good. —*Romans 12:9–21*

Love covers a multitude of sins. Love heals. Love finds. Love waits. Love restores. Love is the source of our power and authority. Love one another. It is the core of all that Jesus taught.

Number Two: Repentance

Repentance is the freedom maker. Jesus offers us repentance and restoration. Hallelujah.

Upon identifying a lie, we confess the lie, repent, and renounce any future practice of sin. Then renounce all agreements and all legal rights of the demonic realm associated with the lie we once believed. We then agree with Jesus and with truth, and finally we stand in truth for ourselves and then for others.

Although we aren't able to override another person's free will, I'm convinced we have biblical examples that allow us to approach the Father and ask for mercy and forgiveness for others. This type of prayer is substitutional repentance. We intercede for others whom we consider inside our jurisdiction. For example, my marriage to Mike is a love covenant and recognized as such by the spiritual realm. From a place of love for my husband, I approach the Father and ask for mercy, forgiveness, and blessing over his life and circumstances. These prayers move the heart of God.

Chapter 9 in the book of Daniel is an example of substitutional repentance. In this chapter we read the confession and repentance prayer that Daniel offered for an entire nation of people. Daniel loved the Hebrew people. And he loved God. His love was at the core of his pleadings. Our love is at the core of our pleadings for ourselves and others.

This is true intercessory prayer. Praying with love in our hearts for the highest and best for another person. This is how we love one another.

A new command I give you: Love one another. As I have loved you, so you must love one another. By this everyone will know that you are my disciples, if you love one another." —John 13:34–35

Number Three: Forgiveness

Be kind and compassionate to one another, forgiving each other, just as in Christ God forgave you. —Ephesians 4:32

A good portion of our journey into wholeness and maturity includes forgiveness. This is the ultimate power weapon that defeats Satan. This includes self-forgiveness, forgiveness of others, forgiving God, and receiving forgiveness through the atonement.

Forgiveness is our restoration process. Restoration and strength are found in the humbling act of forgiving someone who has harmed us. Just as God forgave us, when we choose to forgive others, we release and break the legal rights of the demonic realm.

Evil gains a legal right to torment through unforgiveness, which manifests in emotions such as hate, bitterness, and resentment. When we choose to forgive, we release ourselves from the hatred that binds us to the other person. Wow. This spiritual bazooka will blow up evil oppression and will set us free. It's not always easy, and forgiveness doesn't negate the wrongdoing. Nor does it demand an ongoing relationship with someone who has abused or harmed us. But true forgiveness is the freeing of our own soul and the healing of our heart. Forgiveness opens us up to greater fathoms of God's love, which permeates our hearts and direct our lives.

This is the teaching Jesus provided the disciples in Mark 11. Remember, we are instructed that we may ask anything of God, but Jesus tacks on this sentence at the end of that discourse.

And when you stand praying, if you hold anything against anyone, forgive them, so that your Father in heaven may forgive you your sins. — Mark 11:25

Number Four: Blessing

What is blessing? God blesses. Jesus blesses. But what does it really mean to receive the blessing of God?

Blessing is spiritual empowerment to expand. Cursing is empowering shrinkage. We use our voice, from our secure stance, and we bless others. We release his kingdom of love and power into our world through blessing.

I bless everything. I mean even the small stuff. I bless my home, my relationships, the work of the day ahead. I bless my friendships with love and cooperation. I bless my church, my stubbed toe, and my dogs. I bless my garden, my car, and even the crazy driver who just cut me off. I release the expansion of the Lord's kingdom through blessing. And always in Jesus's name. It's Jesus's authority that I stand behind to give away the love and blessings of our Father.

Blessings are my "go-to" prayers most days. Let me share an example.

Father, today I bless my home with peace. I bless both Mike and myself and my children to live out of divine health. I forbid all evil assignments meant to hinder or hurt me or my family. Lord Jesus, I bless my neighborhood with your love and kindness. I bless the work of my hands and my mind to be strong, and I bless myself to be courageous for your name's sake.

I bless my finances and work opportunities. I bless myself to perceive what you are doing in my life and with common sense to join with you. I bless myself with wisdom, love, and spiritual discernment, and I espe-

cially bless myself with the power to defeat the works of darkness. In your powerful name, Jesus, and by your blood, I ask and bless. Amen.

Joy arises in my heart when I bless. My husband, Mike, always smiles when I bless. And of late, I overhear Mike blessing stuff around the house too. It makes me smile inside when I hear him whisper a blessing in Jesus's name.

Hallelujah!

Forgiveness, repentance, love, and blessing. These are the weapons of our warfare. They are beautiful. They are powerful, and they are life-giving.

For you were once darkness, but now you are light in the Lord. Live as children of light. —Ephesians 5:8

Declare this today aloud: "God is for me. He will work out all things for my good! In Jesus's name, amen!"

PS. Amen means "so be it"!

Ephesians 6
Take up the shield of faith, with which you can extinguish all the flaming arrows of the evil one.

Part Four
Engagements in Spiritual Warfare

I have told you all this so that you may have peace in me. Here on earth you will have many trials and sorrows. But take heart, because I have overcome the world. —John 16:33 (NLT)

Chapter Twelve
SKIRMISHES, BATTLEGROUNDS, AND NUCLEAR WAR

On a Sabbath Jesus was teaching in one of the synagogues, and a woman was there who had been crippled by a spirit for eighteen years. She was bent over and could not straighten up at all. When Jesus saw her, he called her forward and said to her, "Woman, you are set free from your infirmity." Then he put his hands on her, and immediately she straightened up and praised God.
Indignant because Jesus had healed on the Sabbath, the synagogue leader said to the people, "There are six days for work. So come and be healed on those days, not on the Sabbath." The Lord answered him, "You hypocrites! Doesn't each of you on the Sabbath untie your ox or donkey from the stall and lead it out to give it water? Then should not this woman, a daughter of Abraham, whom Satan has kept bound for eighteen long years, be set free on the Sabbath day from what bound her?"
When he said this, all his opponents were humiliated, but the people were delighted with all the wonderful things he was doing.
—Luke 13:10–17

A woman, a child of Abraham (a churchgoer), was bound by Satan for eighteen long years. She was a believer. She was surrounded by people who knew how to set her free but had failed to do so. She remained bound and bent in pain.

Jesus arrives and looks at the infirmity, a spirit, which is wrapped around her.

I often perceive this condition in a person. In Scripture I see this woman as representative of a rebellious lifestyle of her youth, lived far away from God. She is stooped over by the weight of her choices over the years as well as the choices of others that left her with the consequences. Unloving, unkind, or controlling parents, the lack of a father in her life, and dabbling in areas of mischief that lead to evil. Held captive by her sexuality and the ties of old lovers. She's hunched over from the chains of unbelief, pride, and pain. She is plagued by thoughts she will never share with anyone. Shame, guilt, anger, hatred, and bitterness. Death.

When I look at this woman in the Scriptures, I catch sight of her everywhere. Standing on a corner with a sign. A raging husband who rails at his wife and kids. The many lost in a flood of false identities. Those who cry silently with no one to love them. The lonely, sick, disappointed, defeated, and impoverished.

This woman represents all of humanity. Rich and poor. Healthy and sick. Black, white, every ethnicity and nationality. We are walking wounded. Especially those who are yet to be redeemed. I recognize this woman because I was her. I look upon her condition, and I view the hearts of lost mothers and fathers, husbands and wives, best friends, and the prodigal sons and/or daughters who once knew the King.

We need a Savior. We need healing. We need freedom.

The governing powers, religious and demonic, want to keep her bound. Anything miraculous will upset their carefully crafted agendas.

Let me ask you, recruit, do you believe this woman deserves healing? She isn't so different from our unbelieving spouses.

Jesus is astonishingly special in his interaction with her. He knows she is worthy of love. She is worth saving and healing. Compassion overwhelms Jesus as he reaches out and touches her. "Woman, you are set free from your infirmity." She is healed. Released from the lies, the anger, the pain, and in response, she spontaneously praises God.

Cadet, this woman is the unsaved, the walking wounded. We must look past the exterior and ask Jesus to help us perceive and understand the truth of the human before us. When we begin to identify the soul realm issues and pray in alignment with the revelation of their spiritual condition, our prayers enable a hopeful future. Our prayers facilitate healing.

We must decide to push back against the onslaught of cultural lies, deceptions, and untruths. We must draw up our courage and stand upon a battle hill to wage war against everything that is assaulting our loved ones and those who are standing in our jurisdiction.

Common skirmishes emerge as verbal tiffs over political positions, media choices, church attendance, tithing, child rearing. Our beliefs and positions will escalate from an argument to a flammable, passionate battleground. And when challenged, nuclear launch codes are readied as we anticipate Armageddon.

I know because I've been there.

Jurisdiction Hills

Some hills are worth protecting and some are not. Hills worthy to die upon are the core beliefs, which are biblically solid and nonnegotiable. Prayerful consideration and forethought about what issues and beliefs you will die protecting become crucial. Ask for the spirit of Wisdom. Engage this spirit. I'll share more about wisdom later.

There is a time to stand in your truth and engage. And a time to let silence and wisdom reign. Engaging with someone in a rage or a drunken state is futile. Know when and how to set the tone for mature conversation with a spouse or anyone, for that matter. If you don't know, then ask God for a divine setup.

He does this for me all the time.

I pray:

Lord, create an opportunity to talk about [subject] *with* [person]. *Open up the moments when they are willing and open to hear my heart and words. Please make me keenly aware when this moment arrives. Lord, bless me with effective communication that I convey wisdom and truth in a manner they will receive. Help me to listen well. Lord, open their heart to comprehend the truth, and place around us a spirit of unity and cooperation. In Jesus's name, amen.*

Battles in the House and Battles with the Spouse

Determining acceptable behaviors and boundaries is difficult to navigate. Marital boundaries, when well managed, build a strong relationship that cultivates trust, reliability, and vulnerable love. Healthy relationships thrive when established upon healthy boundaries.

After decades of marriage, I know it's wisdom to prayerfully define in your heart the strong boundaries that create a loving marriage relationship. Loyalty, commitment, consideration, honesty, and partnership are several that spring to mind.

For me, I will not abide lying, disloyalty, or abuse in any form, physical, emotional, or spiritual. Working out what is and isn't acceptable is a process. And if you were raised in a home where healthy relationships were not modeled well, then read some good books about healthy relationships, good communication, and effective decision making. Visit a Christian marriage counselor and gain tools for communication and appropriate boundary setting.

Our marriages are the single most significant relationship next to our relationship with the Lord. It's up to us to put the work in even if our spouse refuses. I realize it's not fair. However, someone must. And Jesus chooses you.

My final word on hills to die upon: if your spouse is cheating or abusive, this is not acceptable. Step out of confusion and seek help. Find a trustworthy person to help you process your pain and find a way forward. And it is okay to say to your spouse, "This isn't right. And I deserve to be honored and respected."

Other areas of strong conviction are our children. For me, I would argue a cause for my kids until I'm bloodied, lying in the dirt with arrows all over my back as I protect my youngsters. Dramatic, I know. However, raising my children in church, sharing the Bible with them, allowing them to watch me practice my faith in my home are all nonnegotiable.

Ephesians 6
Take up the shield of faith, with which you can extinguish all the flaming arrows of the evil one.

Chapter Thirteen
EXTERIOR BATTLES: CULTURE

Do not conform to the pattern of this world, but be transformed
by the renewing of your mind. Then you will be able to test and
approve what God's will is—his good, pleasing and perfect will.
—Romans 12:2

Cadet, when you talk about politics and cultural movements with your spouse, does the discussion teeter to becoming explosive? Yep, me too. Why? We are living our values from different worldviews. As believers our view is discerned through the lens of the Word of God. The societal views expressed by our spouse are obtained through a myriad of sources. Science, other religions, cultural practices, etc.—these are ungodly worldviews that are frequently manipulated, garnered by fear and shaming, and they change constantly.

Wisely choose the politics and cultural movements you want to argue. *Know the truth. Stand* in it. You don't have to agree, but *know* in your heart what is right, true, and good. Discern when it's useless to argue, and then pray the issue out with the Lord.

Ask God to intervene, change, rescue, redeem, restore, and battle. He's really good at all of this. And he is absolutely at work to push back evil cultural agendas. Never doubt that for a second.

Over the years I have allowed compromise in my marriage when it comes to small areas of disagreement. For example, for me, church attendance is a must. But Mike, not so much. I attend and he stays home. I'm at peace about going alone.

My spiritual and emotional health is tied to regular attendance among a body of Christian believers. I find encouragement, fulfilment, and love among church members who believe what I believe. It keeps me sane and focused. And corporate worship revives my soul.

Worship is also a warring position. Worship and praise draw the presence of God. Frequently, I will experience a sensation of an angel standing behind me pouring oil over my head. I feel the oil run along my scalp, then drip off the crown of my forehead. Say what?! These moments of worship and communion with God supercharge me. I return home ready to dispatch a few devils back to the pit. Yeah!

Ephesians 6

Take up the shield of faith, with which you can extinguish all the flaming arrows of the evil one.

Chapter Fourteen
EXTERIOR BATTLES: CHURCH

*And let us consider how we may spur one another on toward love
and good deeds, not giving up meeting together, as some are in
the habit of doing, but encouraging one another—and all the
more as you see the Day approaching. —Hebrews 10:24–25*

If you have attended church for more than a few years, it's likely
you've experienced church pain. It's true for nearly all who are
active church members. At some point, arrows of pain, offense, and
misunderstanding penetrate our heart. For us, the unequally yoked, we
face the reality of living as a married single in a couple-dominated
culture—which is a pain category in and of itself. We find ourselves on
the periphery of the church core. And because pastors and the church
body generally lack knowledge of the unique challenges we face in our
marriage and faith, the greater the potential for misunderstanding, poor
advice, and hurt. Sheesh!

We extend grace to our pastors and church body. They are doing the
best they know how.

However, in spite of the challenges, the body of Christ is a miracle
and the answer to our loneliness. We need the church and the church
needs us. As spiritually mismatched believers, we learn to pray. And we

pray with power. Our hearts are filled with compassion, and we are bent toward serving and loving others. We share our distinctive gifting, commitment, and love with our home church. Additionally, our children are impacted, in a positive fashion, through their observation of adults, fathers and mothers, worshiping God and modeling faith and family. Adopting a healthy view of church life helped me tremendously.

I've come to think of church like this. The church is a giant hospital that treats soul sickness, the broken and the dying, physically and spiritually. Incidentally, it's likely we arrived in church as casualties also in need treatment.

Church wounding is real and inevitable as we fellowship alongside damaged people. To become healed and live wholeheartedly, our primary responsibility is to forgive those who wound us and then process our hurts and rejection with Jesus. Allow him to remove our pain and disappointment.

I know of what I'm speaking. I've experienced significant and unfair church wounding, to the point where I physically felt pain in my chest for weeks. Through prayer I asked the Lord to help me process the pain.

I was astonished as he enabled me to perceive the reality of the woman who hurt me. As I caught a glimpse of her walking across the back of the sanctuary one morning, I saw in the spiritual her chest open up, revealing a giant wound the size of her entire chest cavity. She was deeply wounded by her past traumas and therefore lacked the capacity to love or consider the feelings of others.

Once I realized the immense pain she bore, a profound compassion was birthed in me toward her. On the surface, she was beautiful, put together, and a leader in the church community. But Jesus revealed the truth. And I was able to forgive immediately, and then my heart filled with love for her.

Out of our pain, we receive compassion to minister hope and help to others walking the path behind us. Our wounding becomes our greatest weapon against the enemy. Service turns our thoughts away from our lack and irritation to discover wholehearted living through assisting others.

Spiritual Enforcer

The greatest among you will be your servant. —Matthew 23:11

Find a church that lives and breathes Jesus and teaches the Word. Desire to live among a body of believers who will support and love you and your family. Find a place that values vertical worship and participates and desires to manifest the Holy Spirit in their lives.

Jesus is coming for his victorious bride. Make him proud!

Then a voice came from the throne, saying:

"Praise our God, all you his servants, you who fear him, both great and small!"

Then I heard what sounded like a great multitude, like the roar of rushing waters and like loud peals of thunder, shouting:

"Hallelujah!

For our Lord God Almighty reigns.

Let us rejoice and be glad and give him glory!

For the wedding of the Lamb has come,

and his bride has made herself ready.

Fine linen, bright and clean, was given her to wear."

(Fine linen stands for the righteous acts of God's holy people.)

Then the angel said to me, "Write this: Blessed are those who are invited to the wedding supper of the Lamb!" And he added, "These are the true words of God." —Revelation 19:59

Ephesians 6

Take up the shield of faith, with which you can extinguish all the flaming arrows of the evil one.

Chapter Fifteen
EXTERIOR BATTLES: WITCHCRAFT

*For rebellion is as the sin of witchcraft, and stubbornness is as
iniquity and idolatry. —1 Samuel 15:23 (KJV)*

Once a month, like clockwork, Mike and I found ourselves
embroiled in some sort of an absurd disagreement. These arguments would ensue over the stupidest issues. They occurred after dinner
and left us feeling angry and frustrated all evening. The great thing about
our relationship is we are quick to forgive and forget. However, this
cycle wasn't healthy for our relationship. It was so weird!

After a number of these recurring, monthly, idiotic spats, I began to
recognize a clear pattern. This ridiculous fighting strangely occurred with
every full moon. Now, I don't assign any attention to the stars, moon, or
planets. But after asking the Lord about our quarreling, the Lord revealed
that Mike and I were experiencing the effects of witchcraft.

Unfortunately, there are people who partner with darkness. They
participate in spells, rituals, and evil to release demonic beings. Wicca
gather every full moon in the hills or open spaces to practice their incantations and rites. There are numerous gatherings of people who are partnering with dark spirits to release the agendas of evil on humanity. The
darker the gathering, satanic worship, etc., the more these rituals are

directed at Christians, especially families, pastors, and churches with the intention to destroy those of us who worship Yahweh.

I am very sensitive to this realm. Once I recognized this pattern of witchcraft, I simply prayed and placed protection over myself, Mike, and our home. The blood of Jesus became the shield preventing witchcraft from dropping out of the air. Then I reminded Mike that we would not fight on the night of a full moon.

Awareness is a powerful preventive measure.

That's all it took. Awareness and a tiny bit of preparation. When I realize witchcraft is active, I immediately pray something similar to the prayer below. I believe this prayer is straight revelation provided to me from the Lord.

Father, in the name of Jesus, I take authority over all witchcraft, ritual, or any other evil that is spoken or created and aimed at myself, my family, my home, and all that falls under my love, stewardship, and juris- diction. I also stand for those who are under my ministry umbrella [work umbrella, etc]. I hereby cancel all witchcraft spells, rituals, and incanta- tions. Immediately, they must fall to the ground, powerless, and return to those who spoke them with full retribution, until they repent to the true Lord Jesus Christ.

Now I bless myself and all under my authority with angelic protec- tion, the covering of the blood, and the ability to live in faith and joy. In Jesus's name, amen.

Emissaries of evil are no longer in hiding. I've seen witches in churches and at Christian conferences. They are emboldened, now more than ever, because most churchgoers don't know they are among them, let alone how to battle back against spells and incantations.

For many, witchcraft infiltrates through a candle burning, a home sage, crystals, card reading, etc. If you have participated in these seem- ingly harmless practices, repent. Throw it all out and invite the Holy Spirit in. Play worship music, cleanse your home with prayer (find my home-cleansing prayer in Appendix C), and read aloud from the Bible you leave open in the kitchen.

Don't walk with fear. Witchcraft is deceitful. In reality, practitioners are deeply wounded and need love and truth. Pray that they repent to the Lord and discover his love and goodness. Ask the Lord for discernment.

Spellcasting, tarot reading, palm reading, etc. are wide-open doors to demonic oppression and visitation. Find a prayer minister and receive deliverance and freedom.

It is for freedom that Christ has set us free. Stand firm, then, and do not let yourselves be burdened again by a yoke of slavery. —*Galatians 5:1*

Ephesians 6

Take up the shield of faith, with which you can extinguish all the flaming arrows of the evil one.

Part Five
Officer Mind-Set; Victory; Graduation

For "who has known the mind of the Lord that he may instruct Him?"
But we have the mind of Christ. —*1 Corinthians 2:16 (NKJV, emphasis*
mine)

Chapter Sixteen
ENFORCEMENT WISDOM

Out in the open wisdom calls aloud, she raises her voice in the public square; on top of the wall she cries out, at the city gate she makes her speech: "How long will you who are simple love your simple ways? How long will mockers delight in mockery and fools hate knowledge? Repent at my rebuke! Then I will pour out my thoughts to you, I will make known to you my teachings. —
Proverbs 1:20–23

Who Is She?

A number of years ago I became fascinated with Wisdom. In that season, I would walk-n-pray, engaging with her for hours. Wisdom is a female (Proverbs 1) spirit of the Lord (Isaiah 11:2). I read through the book of Proverbs, especially the passages where she is speaking. I discovered she is beautiful, full of grace, patient, and carries the wisdom of the ages.

She longs to instruct God's children in the ways of understanding. She imparts uncommon knowledge and uncanny problem solving. She is present and she is peaceful.

Acquainting myself with Wisdom was one of the best seasons of my life. I spent time in her presence and with the Lord. I was intentionally seeking wisdom that leads to peace. And over time I collected her goodness. I gained prudence and understanding who are also spirits of the Lord. This wisdom is supernatural insight, which will unwind complicated issues and problems. It's training that assists a believer to comprehend past the physical realm and into the spiritual. Partnering with wisdom brought all that is listed in Scripture in the first few chapter of Proverbs and more.

I discovered when walking the path of Wisdom that life's irritants remarkably diminish. I would find that Wisdom would turn up in my conversations with Mike and with others. Wisdom became profoundly interested in my prayer life and the prayer sessions I conducted with others. I recall a conversation with a prayee who just marveled.

She said, "Lynn, you carry such wisdom. This is exactly what I needed to hear and understand."

Of course, it wasn't me. Yet it *was* me. Wisdom lives inside us as the Holy Spirit.

The Lord greatly desires us to live as wise children. He longs to drop creative problem-solving into our minds. He has the answers to every issue humanity is facing. He longs for us to know Wisdom and Prudence. Understanding, along with the remaining Seven Spirits of God, all of which are available to help, instruct, and empower us in life.

When we live with Wisdom, we carry divine perspective and creativity to face difficult decisions and make the best choice. We are provided with heavenly downloads to discern what is actually at hand and stop guessing how to respond to a situation or conversation. Walking with Wisdom leads to living a life of peace.

Be very careful, then, how you live—not as unwise but as wise. — Ephesians 5:15

An example of living life with Wisdom might look like this. On occasions Mike and I would slip into a disagreement regarding any number of topics. In typical fashion we push forward our beliefs and clash over our disagreements. The subjects might include family life, determining who is responsible for the dog's vet visit, or more difficult topics such as politics. Ugh. However, once I began to ask Wisdom to reveal what was really going on, I began to perceive that our arguments were merely the top layer of an altogether different issue.

Turns out that our arguments were actually reflecting either Mike's stress at work, or my insecurity, or the lack of respect one or both of us felt, and the issue at the bottom of it all was fear. Fear would lay concealed under topical subjects, becoming a stoppage point in our communication, thus preventing us from moving forward to resolve our conflicts.

I am somewhat of a risk taker. I have an entrepreneurial spirit that has opened up some significant doors of opportunity and a few amazing successes. I've also experienced a few epic fails. However, most of the time, when I venture into something untried and a bit risky, such as an investment, or travel to a new place, or writing a book, there is an element of risk. What I didn't understand for a long time was that my husband is absolutely risk adverse. He hates the uncomfortable feeling of being unsure about life.

When I would approach him with one of my "ideas," he would argue and provide me with a number of rebuffs to discourage me from moving forward. I lived frustrated and angry for many years. That was until Wisdom began to reveal that our arguments were never about traveling to a new destination or starting something new. Our discord was Mike working his way through the "uncomfortable," aka fear of what the future might hold. Without Wisdom to reveal to me why he was afraid and to show me how to reassure Mike in a way he could accept my ideas, our arguments were futile and frustrating for the both of us.

I *love* Wisdom. With her, I perceive and speak to fear before the beast gains the upper hand. Imagine if the entire church walked in this wisdom today. We would change the world.

When your kids are hurting, Wisdom arrives with the perfect words of comfort and a powerful prayer. She arrives when you've messed up badly and need help to find a way forward out of an impossible situation. Wisdom loves as we ask for divine answers to tremendous problems. She is a portion of our Father's Spirit that releases goodness and life into our circumstance and relationships. Her wisdom is from heaven's perspective and will eclipse worldly wisdom, hands down.

I love the Spirit of Wisdom.

If you haven't engaged with her, open up Proverbs and introduce yourself. Listen to her words. Ask her to come to you and share her perspective. Ask her to instruct you like a tutor. Allow the wisdom of heaven to change you and then abide. Walking with her will change your marriage dynamic and will lead you along the path of righteous living.

I promise. Seek her out! She is a profound gift from our Father.

Neat!

The Spirit of the Lord shall rest upon Him, the Spirit of wisdom and understanding, the Spirit of counsel and might, the Spirit of knowledge and of the fear of the Lord. —Isaiah 11:2 (NKJV)

Ephesians 6

Take up the shield of faith, with which you can extinguish all the flaming arrows of the evil one.

Chapter Seventeen
SETBACKS AND DISAPPOINTMENT

Blessed is the one who perseveres under trial because, having
stood the test, that person will receive the crown of life that the
Lord has promised to those who love him. —James 1:12

It's inevitable: we will experience setbacks. We will meet with disappointment and even failure. After all, we are embroiled in war. We have always been at war and will continue to war until our last breath.

However, each battle, each win or loss ultimately develops our character. We learn from both. Embrace setbacks, whereby we discover forgiveness becomes easier. We gain wisdom and add another tool to our arsenal of weaponry. Even with failure, there is much to be gained for future enforcement activity.

I would like to tell you that even in these later years of my faith walk, I experience fewer setbacks and disappointments. But even within the last couple of years, I walked through Mike's cancer diagnosis and treatment, unexpected delays in our recent move, letdowns in personal relationships and a few other doozies.

Yet I have peace most days. Today I live with the indwelling presence of God that never leaves me. I pray with hundreds of people and bear witness to Jesus releasing freedom and healing into their lives.

This is a profoundly fulfilling way to live out my days.

The years of love and commitment to Jesus, my spouse, and my family have worn away the bristles of conflict. My faith alone wore down my husband's unbelief, and we no longer are at odds about Jesus and all the ministry areas in which I participate. This is a true miracle.

My dear friend, take your pain to Jesus. He is more than enough to comfort and support you. His love fills up the unmet needs that earthly relationships, our marriage, and our family relations are unable or unwilling to fulfill.

This passage in Isaiah is the healing of all our pain, disappointment, illness, and fear:

Surely He has borne our griefs
>*And carried our sorrows;*
>*Yet we esteemed Him stricken,*
>*Smitten by God, and afflicted.*
>*But He was wounded for our transgressions,*
>*He was bruised for our iniquities;*
>*The chastisement for our peace was upon Him,*
>*And by His stripes we are healed.*
>*All we like sheep have gone astray;*
>*We have turned, every one, to his own way;*
>*And the Lord has laid on Him the iniquity of us all. —Isaiah 53:4–6*
(NKJV)

Chapter Eighteen
CAP AND GOWN

Now the serpent was more crafty than any of the wild animals the Lord God had made. He said to the woman, "Did God really say, 'You must not eat from any tree in the garden'?" —Genesis 3:1

C adet, as commencement draws nigh, let's consider the most important aspect of a powerful enforcement officer of the King. *Did God really say . . . ?*

The questioning of God's voice is as old as time. Enforcers, we *must* know our Lord's voice and know his character because the days of evil are upon us. For many, we face the questions, accusations, and ridicule of our beliefs and faith right in our own home. We have shouldered perseverance among the shaming and persecution.

We have now obtained a *stance* of faith that empowers and affirms. But one day in the future, the enemy will subtly rise up against you. He will not come with clubs and obvious battle approaches. No, he will simply ask a question.

Did God say you have power and authority? Are you able to fully protect your home inside and out? Do you believe you will enforce the truth amid the onslaught of faulty cultural narratives, distortions of identity, and fear of ridicule?

Did God really say that your past shame and guilt are completely wiped away? Did God say you are worthy to be loved, honored, and respected?

Did God really say . . . ?

This question may arise from our spouse, a trusted family member, a person who bears great importance and influence in our lives, or from the culture that is railing against all things holy. Supported by seemingly convincing arguments, their sarcasm and the pressure to surrender weighs heavily upon our badge of faith.

But never doubt that we are equipped and battle ready. We shall arise and stand in our full stature upon the unchanging Word of God. Upon the powerful voice of our good Father, who has been speaking to his people for millennia. The voice that remains as steadfast and true today as it was more than two thousand years ago. It is truth and it is life.

My dear, dear friend, the rebuttal to every question aimed your way by evil is what God says. Let the truth defend you and your identity be your response:

Simply reply: "This is what my Father says about me . . ."

I am the head and not the tail.

I was created for greatness.

I am beautiful and wonderfully made.

I am a coheir with Christ Jesus.

I am a leader and not a follower.

I am a Holy Ghost–demon-sniper.

I am chosen.

I love God.

I love people.

I am a friend of God.

I am a godly woman/man.

I am important.

I am filled with the wisdom of heaven.

I have a divine destiny.

My purpose is extreme and powerful.

I have a legacy of faith.

I am the righteousness of Christ Jesus.

I am a beloved child of God.

I am above only and not below.

I am empowered.

I am prayerful.

I am strong and courageous.

I am faith filled.

I am worthy.

I am enough.

I am victorious.

I am loved.

My dear friend, the absolute truest thing about you is that you are loved. These are the answers to every question the enemy has ever propagated. These statements are scripturally based and are the words that define you.

We will no longer shrink back from the truth of what our Father says about us. From this day forward, we stand under the armor of God, aligned, espousing faith and belief, championing the Word of God to evil agents and snatching our family members from the flames of hell.

We will not relent. We will not go silently. We will not listen to the liar.

We will stand shoulder to shoulder in the fight, waging war for the redemption of souls. It is our time. This is our mission. And we will not fail.

All of heaven is waiting for the sons and daughters of God to arise and step into their mature and powerful identity. The great cloud of witnesses watches as we swing our swords to cut down demons and release hope, love, and a future to entire generations to finally birth a kingdom renaissance.

Hallelujah.

Stand tall, cadet. We have our Father on our side. And his kingdom is here to advance with us. We are the humble mothers, fathers, grandparents, and citizens who are commissioned for this, the great end-times battle.

We are equipped, mandated, fully capable, and ready to bring his kingdom on earth as it is in heaven. Amen.

Ephesians 6

Take up the shield of faith, with which you can extinguish all the flaming arrows of the evil one.

Chapter Nineteen
COMMENCEMENT

For everyone born of God overcomes the world. This is the victory that has overcome the world, even our faith. —1 John 5:4

Congratulations!
Today is graduation day. Take a moment and soak it all in. Contemplate and celebrate everything that you have gained to live victoriously.

Receive your badge. Wear it proudly. I suggest you buy a cross necklace. It's the cross of Christ that provides the authority to triumph in life. I wear a cross around my neck, and I also wear a bracelet, which has three small round beads followed by a long silver bead, representing three dots and a dash: . . . — Again, this is Morse code for "Victory"! I smile every time I put it on.

Kingdom enforcer, find a symbol that holds meaning specific to your faith life. Wear it as your badge of confidence, knowing the unseen realm acknowledges the symbol that represents the power and authority you live from.

Take up your weapons, the Ephesians 6 mantel of faith. Each weapon is mighty to the destruction of evil and the rescue, healing, and salvation of every person in your jurisdiction. We serve the almighty, powerful God. It's for His name we stand and we pray. Hallelujah.

Linger in his presence. Rejoice in the Lord always. Live a life worthy of his calling.

Graduate, the classroom has concluded. Thank you for pouring yourself into this study and sharing this journey with me. I know that the principles I've shared are powerful and they work. They will help you.

It's my heart's desire that you live in the fullness of all the Lord has determined for your life and family.

God is good. So are you, and I truly love you. I know one day we will share our stories with one another. I long for that day with great anticipation.

I bless you, my dear brother or sister in the Lord. I bless you with courage. I bless you with hope. I bless you with strength and a sound mind. I bless you with persistence and belief that moves mountains. I bless you to be a demon slayer and to rescue your family from evil. I bless you to know who you are and whose you are. I bless you to walk with the power and authority of Jesus. I bless you to manifest the Holy Spirit. And I bless you to love. Love God and love people. I pray all of this with a full heart. In the mighty name of our Savior, Jesus Christ our Lord, amen!

[Jesus said,] "I have told you these things, so that in me you may have peace. In this world you will have trouble. But take heart! I have overcome the world." —John 16:33

Spiritual Enforcer

Ephesians 6

Take up the shield of faith, with which you can extinguish all the flaming arrows of the evil one.

Chapter Twenty

VICTORY

But thanks be to God! He gives us the victory through our Lord
Jesus Christ. —1 Corinthians 15:57

Three dots and a dash . . . — After seeing these unusual clouds in the sky and looking up their meaning, the song "The War Is Over" by Bethel Music sprang to mind. I found the song on my music app and listened to the lyrics as it played from my phone.

I burst into tears! I *knew* it was finally over. It was my time to lay the weapons on the ground. The waiting, the longing, the battles on the home front. I knew financial provision and peace were emerging following the long years of warring for the truth, our finances, and Mike's salvation.

This is the overwhelming victory that is ours. We are children in the arms of peace. We are sons and daughters, and we belong. We are filled with power and authority, and we are always enough.

I wept and walked, my spirit completely overwhelmed by the love and affirmation of the Father. It all came rushing back to my memory. The years I stood in a shaky but determined faith stance. All that I believed and hoped for and all the evil I'd warred against. And oh, how I loved.

What Is Victory?

Cadet, what does victory look like?

It's a fall afternoon here in Northern California, and a few years have passed since the three dots and dash appeared in the sky. I'm writing from my favorite spot in the house. Glancing out the window, I catch the beauty of yellow leaves falling in a gentle, wispy twirl. I look past the leaves and catch sight of a skittish doe searching for carrots I left along our backyard fence. It's my perfect gift. A gift from my Father. A gift I've waited decades to receive and one I didn't even know I desired with all of my heart.

When I sign a book, I always include Psalm 37:4 as a scripture reference. I hope readers have looked it up.

Delight yourself also in the Lord, and He shall give you the desires of your heart. —Psalm 37:4 (NKJV)

The life I live today is the result of God's faithfulness, and this life *is* the desire of my heart. I'm harvesting the fruit of extreme perseverance in prayer and faith for the outcomes I once thought impossible. I have walked nearly six decades with God. And I know this for certain: he is good. He truly loves us, deeply.

Our Father cares about the smallest details in our life and longs to intercede if we would just get out of the way. He has a wonderful future for us and our family. He will never give up hoping and waiting for us to align with him and make a path for others to find him.

He owns the cattle on a thousand hills. He lavishes his provision and love. He blesses, restores, and heals, despite the fact we forget to thank him.

I am the happiest I have ever been in my entire life. Did life turn out as I hoped or expected? Definitively no. But it's beautiful.

In this season I'm often asked, would you do it again? Would you marry an unbeliever? This is my answer.

I would walk all of the difficult years again. I would cry, I would pray, I would hope and then do it all again, year upon year, if the result was my life as it is today.

The most important part of my entire life experience was gaining a love relationship with God and learning to love people. I wouldn't trade God for anything in the world. I hear his voice, and I live a fulfilling and wholehearted life.

I live in a home that is way above my pay grade. My husband and I are in love and live in peace. We really know one another. He is the echo to my life here on Planet Earth, as I am to his.

There is something uniquely intimate, special, and holy about living a life of marriage with an imperfect person. I've learned to forgive. I've learned compassion. I've gained intimacy with the Holy Spirit, the spirit of Wisdom, and I know Jesus as my everything.

I know the Bible is true, and it is powerful It IS the very voice of God. I've participated in supernatural and unexplainable circumstances that have blown my mind and stirred up my hunger for more.

I've prayed until I've wept. I've grieved over prodigals and the choices of others. I've whined to God. I've pleaded. I've rejoiced with so much thanksgiving I thought my heart would pop out of my chest and float up to heaven.

There has been pain. There is disappointment. But there is redemption and restoration, and there is so much love. This is the imperfect, unexpected, yet fully divine life. This is holiness.

This is the life of the believer. This is the truth that we have from the Scriptures. God is faithful.

And in response, we are faithful. We will respond to our mandate with conviction and passion as long as we have breath.

Heal the sick, cleanse the lepers, raise the dead, cast out demons. Freely you have received, freely give. —Matthew 10:8 (NKJV)

My war at home is over. Mostly. *grin*

I continue to fight the good fight for my family, and I war for you, my brothers and sisters. I cry for you. I rejoice with you. I love you, and I care deeply about your spiritual development. I will not grow weary. My war cry is "Victory!"

Write to me when you can. Share your stories with me. May your victorious life bring honor to the name of Jesus, the Christ, the son of the living God.

Love and hugs,

Lynn

Fear not, for I am with you;

Be not dismayed, for I am your God.

I will strengthen you,

Yes, I will help you,

I will uphold you with My righteous right hand. —*Isaiah 41:10 (NKJV)*

Appendix A
HEALING PRAYER WITH LYNN DONOVAN

To schedule a healing or deliverance prayer, visit https://www.lynndonovan.com/healing-prayer.html

Healing prayer is a focused two hours of prayer over the phone. Through prayer, we seek Jesus and the Holy Spirit to lead us into all truth (John 16:13). It's completely confidential and *powerful*! You will find the truth about who God is and who you are. More importantly, you will leave peaceful, feeling joy and filled with blessings. You will be released into a new season with the Savior, Jesus Christ, and find peace, healing, and *freedom*!

Appendix B
Spiritual Mentoring with Lynn Donovan

Spiritual mentoring is one-to-one coaching and discipleship. These sessions are intended to further develop the spiritual, emotional, physical life of the Christian believer. At times there is homework assigned. To schedule, visit https://www.lynndonovan.com/accelerate-your-journey-faith-mentorship.html

Topics of Study

Attributes of a Mature Child of God:

Intimacy Opens the Gates of Heaven:
Tired of praying powerless prayers? There is a different way to pray, and it begins with "first fruits." This study will deepen your relationship with each member of the Trinity. You will discover how to pray differently as you relate to the Father, Son, and Holy Spirit.

Engaging the Angels:
Scriptural study of angels, understanding their function, their destiny and how it's tied to our own. Their power, authority, and purposes. The various types of angelic beings. Interacting with the angelic. Engaging

the angelic in your life, prayers, Courts of God and more. Listening and engaging with angels.

The Reality of Demons:

Scriptural study. Jesus's interactions with the demonic. His ministry is our ministry. Our authority in the demonic realm. The Occult. How that realm gains stronghold in our lives and learn how we become free from it. Detecting witchcraft. Defeating the demonic. Learning to deliver yourself and others from demons.

The Power of Your Voice:

The voice of a child of God carries great power and authority. Discover how the devil has stolen our voice and how to gain it back. We will also focus on using our voice in cooperation with heaven and praying with a powerful voice.

Hearing God's Voice:

Everyone can hear God. So why don't we sometimes? We must learn how to tune in, how to remove blockages. In this topic you will clear your ears and eyes, develop your spiritual sight, sanctify your imagination, and learn how to steward God's voice and his words.

Divine Healing:

Physical healing is complex. There are several components that we must understand to step into this area of healing with Jesus. What is spiritual or merely physical? This topic will focus on understanding when we need to engage the power of the Holy Spirit for a creative miracle versus dealing with a demon of infirmity. What is divine health? How do we apprehend it for ourselves and others? You will learn how to pray for healing for self and others.

Lifestyle of a Powerful Child of God:

This study will emphasize what this lifestyle is and what it is not. We learn what this lifestyle offers to believers. How to consistently live as a child of God. (Everyone needs this training. You can't step into greater realms in the kingdom without understanding this.)

Speaking in Tongues:

What are tongues, according to the Bible? Why and how is it used? What happens in the spiritual realm when we pray in our heavenly prayer language? Activation if you want to receive this gift. What is an open heaven?

Gifts of the Spirit:

What is a seer? What is the seer realm? Who has this gift? How to seek and receive this gifting. Proper protocols to operate in this gifting. What is the Feeler gift? And Gifts of dreams and visions.

Prophetic Gifts:

What is a prophetic gift? Discover the differing manifestations of this gift. Learn how to step into this Holy Spirit gift. Understanding proper protocols and responsibilities when operating in this gift. Prophetic words, feelings, signs, dreams, visions, art, and creativity. Connection with the Holy Spirit and the purpose of living from this gifting. Joy, hope, divine purpose, *love*.

The Power of the Blood of Christ and Communion:

In this session we will learn about what really happened at the cross and what Jesus went through to bring us into the most powerful covenant offered to humanity. Communion is more than a mere symbol. We will explore the power behind communion as well. Also covered will be the process to rid ourselves of ugly images, such as pornography, in our mind.

Praying in the Throne Room:

Approaching the Mercy Seat. Attitudes, permissions, gates. The atmosphere. Who is there? What God is doing? Jesus, Spirit, and others. How we receive grace and mercy in His Presence.

Engaging the Words of God:
Recognizing the depths of God's Word. Uncovering the treasures that belong to you in the Bible. How to apply the Word as a tool for victory and overcoming evil. How to claim the promises and watch them come into fruition in your life.

A Holiness Lifestyle:
Is it obtainable today? How, what, when, and where. The rewards of holiness and the tremendous access it grants.

Kingdom Legalities:
Covenants, Contracts, hidden documents, blueprints, and the legalities of freedom and freeing those who are imprisoned.

Sexual Spirits—Incubi and Succubae:
Sexual spirits are rampant in our society and culture. Uncover how they gain entrance and how to cast them out with all their effects. You are provided with power and authority to remove the plagues of sexual sin from your life and the lives of others.

The Devil's Endgame:
End times.

Be prepared to take notes, look up scriptures, and learn the practical application regarding each of these topics. I have experience teaching these topics to church groups, prayer ministries, and online ministry training. Always look to Jesus, the author and finisher of our faith, to equip and reveal truth.

Appendix C
HOME CLEANSING PRAYER

Excerpt from *My Child Sees Monsters* by Ann Marie Mora and Lynn Donovan

Ann Marie: I started this epic and unprecedented adventure of spiritually cleansing my home by opening every door and window in the entire house, as recommended by Lynn. Next, I grabbed my essential oil, blessing it in Jesus's name, and then sat down silently on the floor, one room at a time. I invited the Holy Spirit into the room. I prayed, asking the Holy Spirit if there was anything that was unholy or that opposed the love of Jesus. In each room I discerned a picture or heard a word in my head identifying something in the room that was not right. I picked it up, threw it out, and then recited this prayer:

Father, I come boldly and confidently into your presence, and I stand in authority in this house and in this room. I now cast out any demonic thing or activity that is not of you. I send it to the foot of the cross. It cannot return, nor retaliate against me or my family members. It can't ask for help on the way out. In Jesus's mighty name.

Then I blessed each room with family unity, good communication, bold conversations, love, and anything more I sensed was needed, and always in the name of Jesus.

Visit MyChildSeesMonsters.com for more information regarding *My Child Sees Monsters* by Ann Marie Mora and Lynn Donovan.

Appendix D
IDOL WORSHIP LIST

God detests idol worship. Detest is the strongest word in the Bible. God hates rebellion. As his followers, it's our highest responsibility to have no other gods before him. Below is a list of practices or beliefs that are potentially open doors to sin and oppression. The list is merely made available to you as a prayer reference. If you have been involved in any of these areas, depending on your commitment and participation, you may be experiencing oppression and strongholds. Remember, it's the heart response that allows a door to open to the demonic. Ask yourself, Is it possible that I've assigned any supernatural power or advantage to something outside my faith in God? If so, simply repent and confess. Confession and repentance release you from evil entanglements. Remember, I am only a messenger. Some of the items below may surprise you.

Do your research. I've researched many practices such as yoga, chiropractic, acupuncture, and discovered their origin is rooted in Eastern Mysticism.

Also remember, if you are a child of God and have been saved through the blood of Christ, all of these *must* bow to the name of Jesus Christ.

Pray aloud:

Father, in the name of Jesus, I confess that I have knowingly or unknowingly offered my heart, my belief, or my hope to any god other than you. I grieve that I have rebelled against your wise statutes, and I have hurt your heart. I repent for participating in any way physically, with my body. I repent for offering my soul or spirit to any foreign god. I ask for your forgiveness for _____ [insert specifics and pray as the Holy Spirit leads].

I also confess and ask for forgiveness on behalf of my ancestors for any way they participated in idol worship. Please forgive all of us. Please cleanse our family name and forgive our blood guilt. I now apply the blood of Jesus to these sins, and I receive the forgiveness that he purchased on my behalf. I also receive his healing and freedom. Now reunite me into your heart, Father.

Holy Spirit, lead me to depend on the power and love of the Father wholly and faithfully as my only source for help, protection, provision, love, and acceptance.

I pledge my loyalty, my love, my service here on earth and eternally to you, Father. In the mighty, saving name of Jesus, amen!

Black-and-white magic
Witchcraft
Wiccan
Wizards
Psychic reading
Psychic prayers
Enchantments
Spells
Fortune telling
Tarot cards
Necromancy
Divination/Python Spirit
Potions
Ouija Boards

Crystals and crystal balls
Bloody Mary
The Bell Witch
Charlie Charlie
Red Door, Yellow Door
Kundalini
Echankar
Yoga
Kabbalah
Mind-emptying meditation
Transcendental meditation
Reincarnation
ESP
Chanting
Seances
Levitation
Astrology
Zodiac
Horoscopes
Idolatry
Acupuncture
Sorcery
Satanism
Satanic Ritual Abuse
Animal/human sacrifice
Alchemy
Pentagram
Enneagram
Imaginary friends
Karma
Voodoo
Demon Baphomet
Witch doctors
Light as a Feather, Stiff as a Board
Reiki

Martial arts
Hypnosis
Astral projection
Shape shifting
Palm reading
Clairvoyance
Channeling
Trolls
Charms
Amulets
Conjuring
Incantations
Yin Yang
Tattoos
Graven images
Covens
Ungodly music
Horror movies
Halloween
Tea leaves
Coffee grounds
Table tipping
Dream catchers
Mediums
Oaths/covenants
Hexes/vexes
Grave sucking
Spirit guides
Soul travel
Metaphysics
Telekinesis
Telepathy
Poltergeists
Angel worship
Goddess

Dungeons and Dragons
Pokemon
Aneme
Freemasons
Eastern Star
Order of the Rainbow
DeMolay
Odd Fellows
Order of the Arrow
Secret societies of any kind
Superstition
Familiar spirits
Ancestral spirits
Spiritualism
Indigo
Incense
Sage
Automatic handwriting

For a full list and prayers for freedom from religious spirits, sexual spirits, spirits of infirmity, and more, visit https://www.lynndonovan. com/free-stuff.html

Appendix E
FALSE RELIGIONS/RELIGIOUS SPIRITS

Pray through the list below using the prayer above in Appendix D.

Eastern mysticism

Legalism

Denominational spirits

Lukewarm

Scientology

Confucianism

Zen

Buddhism

Babylonian spirits

Falsehood

Compromise

Rastafarianism

Anarchy

Biorhythm

Shamanism

Apostasy

Universalism

Pantheism

I Ching

Taoism
Islam
Spirits: Greek Mythology
Shintoism
Hinduism
Kali
Saraswati
Ganesha
Shiva
White supremacy
KKK
Paganism
Native American spiritualism
False tongues/false gifts
Antichrist Spirit
Antisemitism
Black Muslim
New Age practices
Earth worship
Spirit of Error
Krishna
Blasphemy
Unitarianism
Mormonism
Spiritualism
Unification Church
Atheism
Christian Science
Jehovah Witnesses
Demonic Doctrines
Humanism

Appendix F
RECOMMENDED READING

Marching Around Jericho: Praying Your Unsaved Spouse into the Kingdom, Lynn Donovan (2019)

I Give You Authority: Practicing the Authority Jesus Gave Us, Dr. Charles H. Kraft (2012)

They Shall Expel Demons: What You Need to Know a out Demons—Your Invisible Enemies, Derek Prince (2020)

The Unseen Realm: Recovering the Supernatural Worldiew of the Bible, Dr. Michael S. Heiser (2015)

Other Titles by Lynn Donovan:

Winning Him Without Words: 10 Keys to Thriving in Your Spiritually Mismatched Marriage, Lynn Donovan and Dineen Miller (2011)

Raising Godly Kids in a Spiritually Mismatched Home: 10 Keys to Teaching Your Children to Love God Without Limits!, Lynn Donovan and Dineen Miller (2017)

Winning Them with Prayer: Prayer Strategies for the Spiritually Mismatched, Lynn Donovan and Dineen Miller (2017)

Kingdom Conversations: 90 Devotions for Those Who Are Listening for the Voice of God, Lynn Donovan (2020)

Other resources by Lynn Donovan:

LynnDonovan.com

MarchingAroundJericho.com

SpirituallyUnequalMarriage.com

Ephesians 6

Take up the shield of faith, with which you can extinguish all the flaming arrows of the evil one.

"Blessed are You, Lord God of Israel, our Father, forever and ever.
Yours, O Lord, is the greatness,
The power and the glory,
The victory and the majesty;
For all that is in heaven and in earth is Yours;
Yours is the kingdom, O Lord,
And You are exalted as head over all.
Both riches and honor come from You,
And You reign over all.
In Your hand is power and might;

In Your hand it is to make great
And to give strength to all.
"Now therefore, our God,
We thank You
And praise Your glorious name.
—1 Chronicles 29:10–13 (NKJV)

Read Lynn's Other Books

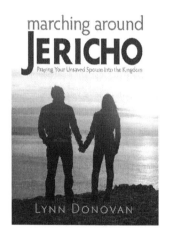

Marching Around Jericho
by Lynn Donovan

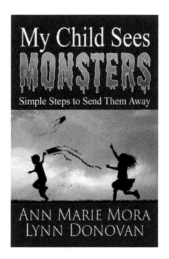

My Child Sees Monster
by Lynn Donovan and Ann Marie Mora

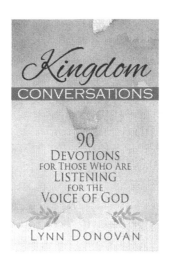

Kingdom Conversations
by Lynn Donovan

Spiritual Enforcer

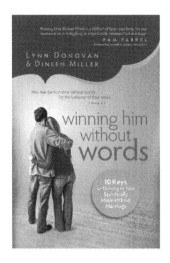

Winning Him Without Words
by Lynn Donovan & Dineen Miller

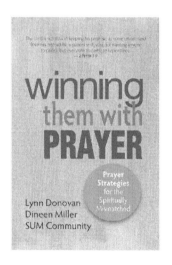

Winning Them with Prayer
by Lynn Donovan & Dineen Miller

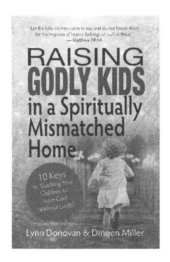

Raising Godly Kids
by Lynn Donovan & Dineen Miller

LYNNDONOVAN.COM

Made in the USA
Columbia, SC
24 May 2025